The

Dave

Maynard

Spin

By

Dave Maynard

As told to

Suzan Franks

Rosstrum Publishing

Nashua, NH

Also by Dave Maynard

Dave Maynard's Soups, Stews and Casseroles

Dave Maynard's Tried and True All-Night Radio Secret Family

Recipe Cookbook

Dave Maynard's Beginnings & Endings and a Whole Bunch of

Breads in the Middle (Ed)

Also available from Rosstrum Publishing

Fast Track for Caregivers

Lawless in Brazil

366 Tips for a Successful Job Search

Timberline

Pursuit

How to Improve your Interviewing Skills

Coming soon:

Dr. Lawless, I Presume

Cedar Canyon

Journey of a Beam: A 9-11 Pictorial Remembrance

Visit www.rosstrumpublishing.com for details

Rosstrum Publishing books are available at discount when purchased in bulk for premiums and sales promotions as well as for fundraising or educational use. Based on quantities, special editions can be created to specification. For details, contact the publisher by mail or by e-mail.

This book represents the memories and recollections of Dave Maynard. Neither the authors nor publisher is responsible for the content contained herein.

Rosstrum Publishing
8 Strawberry Bank Road
Suite 20
Nashua, NH 03062-2763
RosstrumPublishing@gmail.com
www.rosstrumpublishing.com

Library of Congress Control Number: 2012943834

Manufactured in the United States of America
First printing July, 2012
1 3 5 7 9 10 8 6 4 2

To my children and step-children – Michael, Meredith, Marney, Mark, Megan, Matthew, Debra, and John – who had to put up with my long working hours; and to my loyal listeners who made it all possible.

Acknowledgments

I want to express my deep appreciation to our publisher, Joseph Ross of Rosstrum Publishing for his valuable input and help editing this wonderful book. I am thankful for his confidence in the book and the encouragement that has been so helpful to me during the publishing process.

I would also like to thank Beverley Whipple, for her help inserting the initial photos in the book, which adds to your enjoyment of each story. Nic Zateslo offered wonderful advice and assistance in the establishment and maintenance of the **Dave Maynard Spin** web site. Also a big thanks to Jill O'Brien for helping to edit the first draft of the book, and to Carol Noll and Ann Cohen for their encouragement and support in helping to get this book published. I would also like to thank Bill Aydelott, producer of Waverly Motion Pictures, who gave us the "Dave's Piece o' Cake" TV commercials that we posted on Dave's Facebook site. A big thank you to my son Justin who made the Internet useable, to my son Robbie Smith, and to all my good friends, who encouraged me. Their encouragement kept me going because they knew just how much I believed in this book and the history, humor, substance, and value it offered to everyone who reads it.

S.F.

The

Dave

Maynard

Spin

Dave Maynard

As told to Suzan Franks

Table of Contents

Foreword

On a wonderful 85 degree day, I was sitting poolside in Florida, waiting for some friends. I set my towels on three chaise lounges next to an older, good-looking man and sat down to wait. When a third friend showed up, I realized I did not have enough lounges for all of them.

Suddenly, my neighbor said, "I can move over a chaise to make room for your friends."

I was about to decline, when I had to do a double-take. That voice – that unforgettable voice – was embedded in my memory. Without thinking, I blurted out, "Who are you? You're famous."

He smiled like the Cheshire cat and finally said, "I'm Dave Maynard."

"Wow," I replied. "You're Dave Maynard. WBZ, Boston." I fairly gushed, "I listened to you every morning on the radio from the time I was four years old. I am *so* pleased to meet you."

When I came home, I told practically everyone I know: my husband, my parents back in Marblehead, Mass., my sister, who also lives in Marblehead, my older kids in New Hampshire, my youngest son in Florida, and everyone else I could think of. *Holy Cow!* I thought. I was thrilled to meet an accomplished celebrity who lived here in my own neighborhood.

Four months later, I was collecting signatures to run for the Florida State Senate. When I rang one doorbell, I was shocked when the door was opened by Dave Maynard. "Hi, Dave," I blurted.

Without waiting for the reason I was there, he invited me in and offered me a cold drink. More than an hour passed while he regaled me with stories of the people he had met during his radio and television days in Boston. I was fascinated with his humorous stories and I hung on every word. I could close my eyes and listen to his voice – that amazing voice.

After that election (which I lost), I said to my husband, "I think I would like to write down the stories Dave told me, so the family can pass them down to the grandchildren. Do you think he would let me do it?"

My husband smiled and said, "Well, you won't know unless you ask."

About 2 ½ years and about 64,000 words later, *The Dave Maynard Spin* was born. When we had collaborated on around two-thirds of the book, Dave said he would like to see the book published.

These stories are heartwarming. Many are hilarious. They are a tribute to a lifetime spent working in radio and television. Many who remember those times would say the effort was, "a piece of cake." The stories range from Dave's time spent as a private eye to his interviews of some of the most prominent statesmen in the world, much of it filled with the wit and humor he was quick to share with us all.

In addition, he tossed in some classic one-liners and even a few health tips. In some cases, we had to change the names to protect the innocent . . . or not so innocent.

Working with Dave on this book was like attending the Dave Maynard School of Broadcasting. I watched tapes of some hysterical commercials: Challenging Boston Celtics great, Robert Parrish, to a one-on-one basketball competition; a boxing match with middleweight champion, Marvelous Marvin Hagler; and Dave in drag, exercising with Richard Simmons. All promoted *Maynard in the Morning*, his WBZ radio program.

There were trunks full of photos documenting 22 years of traveling the world, leading tours. In addition, there were hundreds of pages of jokes he used, newspaper and magazine articles, and the many recognitions and awards he won over the years. The single element Dave had in abundance was passion; passion for the music, passion for his curiosity, passion which showed through his energy, the energy of at least eight men.

During the preparation of this book, I was uplifted by his gift of gab, his dry humor, his enrichment of lives by reading, listening and remembering his words.

You will be too.

Suzan Franks

Introduction

The Dave Maynard Spin is a compilation of nearly 50 years of humorous and historical recollections by the legendary and beloved radio and television personality and author, Dave Maynard, starting with the heyday of New England radio to the mid-1990s.

The manuscript includes unique personal interviews which feature some of the 20th and 21st century's most important cultural figures, including such luminaries (not to name-drop) as the legendary "Fats" Domino, Julia Child, Louis Armstrong, Tony Bennett, Andy Williams, Richard Simmons, Nat King Cole, Warren Beatty, Paul Newman, Tip O'Neill and Prime Minister Benjamin Netanyahu, just to name a few.

As a worldwide traveler for 22 years, Dave gives the reader an intriguing look at his experiences as leader of the first tour groups allowed to visit both Russia and China, as well as many other captivating adventures to foreign lands. As host of the television show, Community Auditions (often referred to as the precursor to Star Search), he shares a few stories from that live telecast that are sure to entertain. It also includes chapters on politics, including a story on payola in the record industry, and his testimony before the U.S. Congress. In a chapter called *Beantown and Beyond*, he recalls a story about playing with the Boston Celtics and a $5 million contract offer by Red Auerbach. In addition, the book includes a chapter on *Dave's Health Tips* that former listeners continue to request. A chapter on *Humor*, includes a series of one liners for the would-be standup comic, or anyone who is just looking for a good laugh. A chapter named *Words to Live By* includes some humorous and helpful hints for life's challenges; a chapter entitled *Star Spotters*, and a chapter named *Pearls of Wisdom*, all written with that special Dave Maynard flair, prove to the reader, there really *is* humor in almost everything. The final chapter of this book ends with a poem written by a long time radio fan extolling the miracle of Dave Maynard's birth, that will bring the reader to a laugh-out-loud conclusion. All of these items are culled from actual broadcasts.

Some of the photos in the book may seem fuzzy. Unfortunately, that is how we started. We felt it was worth it to include them anyway.

Dave's big break in broadcasting started at a new station, WHIL, where he was fortunate enough to land his first big interview – with Louis Armstrong. To help you learn the flavor of Dave's personality, this book starts with Dave's college career where – just perhaps – he learned the ways of the world.

The

Dave

Maynard

Spin

Chapter 1

The Stories of Sherlock Maynard

"Turn down the volume of your set because it's time for the trials and tribulations of Sherlock Maynard."

Sherlock Maynard in College

You might think this chapter of my life would be off-limits. After all, everyone does unexpected, if not crazy things, in their post-secondary-school lives, but in this instance I wanted to share some of my job-related know-how, working my way through college as a Private Eye.

My First Assignment

Just what is so great about Dick Tracy? I'll have you know that sheer bravado was exhibited quite a number of times in the early 1950s by yours truly. Let's take, for example, the first assignment given to me by the William J. Burns International Detective Agency. The perp was a middle-aged man who spent at least three nights a week at an Irish barroom in Dorchester, MA. In this case the perp was the bartender. If you are from that area of the country, I'm talking about "Daachestah." In my briefing, I had it pounded into my head, "Don't Tip," which meant don't blow your cover. I've always preferred Ivy League clothing, but this was not that type of barroom.

It was February, and I had on a turtleneck sweater, corduroy slacks, a tweed overcoat, and my buckskin shoes. I looked terrible for an undercover agent, but nobody stared at me, so I slid into a stool at the bar and ordered a beer. I must say that I was puffed up with my own brilliance when the guy on the stool next to me, turned to me and, with brotherly love, said, "Hello," . . . just that, "Hello." . . . This was an important step, as I quickly started up a conversation with him to pass the time while drinking my beer.

Now I want to bring you up-to-date on my sleuthing. I forgot to mention the people who owned the bar were suspicious of the perp's activities. I made a kind of study of his activities, and I made a study of him as well. I became a bit worried, because in those days I didn't drink very much alcohol, and I began to feel the effects on me after the first two beers. Luck was on my side though, because before I became a little dippy, I observed exactly what had cast suspicion on the bartender.

I felt that I had to be very careful when talking to the guy next to me. I could just imagine what hell could break loose if it got around the bar that a college kid was there trying to get the goods on the bartender.

Lucky for me, he clipped the bar register several times. Let me tell you how he did it. He only took money when he was making change for somebody who was paying a bar bill in cash. He had a swift little move as he rang up the total and turned to the customer. He had a way of shaving the bill and pocketing the change. I drank three beers and realized the time for me to go was . . . now. So all that was left to do was to go back to my apartment and write up a report. So much for trying to clip the register. I'm proud to say that I learned to drink beer in that one night, and also that I didn't get my block knocked off!

Flushed with success, I received a call from the Burns Detective Agency asking me if I would like to do another surveillance job, and I, of course replied, "Yes." They told me that this would be a two-man job, and that intrigued me. I was introduced to my sleuthing cohort and I could never forget his name . . . Joc Fallon. What a great name for a Detective. He was also a student from Emerson College. We were given a briefing and, two days later, we went on the job. Joe started by watching the back entrance of Jordan Marsh in Boston, I was across the street looking in the windows of Filene's. We found out in the briefing that this was to be a long and short tail. That means, when you're covering somebody, the long tail is a good distance away, and the short tail is close up. The reason for this was that I had never seen the suspected perpetrator, but Joe had, and he was to finger the suspect I needed to follow. Now for the interesting part: the man we were to tail all afternoon had a curious habit. His job was selling men's suits at Jordan's. He was alleged to have a pesky habit; he would take a suit off the rack, don the items of clothing in the dressing room at the end of his shift and then wear his own clothing over the new suit, walk out the door, and head home.

Joe Fallon crossed the street, approached me and we spoke a bit; in fact we spoke too much I think, as you will soon find out. It was near the end of shift time for the store and Boston's downtown would be stuffed with people, making it tougher to trail the perp. The two of us were looking at some window display, waiting for the successful swiper. Then Joe said, "There he is. . . . Turn Around!" which I did. Believe it or not, there must have been seven or eight guys looking in that display window alongside me. Yet I felt apprehensive because we were the only people who knew a theft was in progress. My senses were keen and I was acutely aware of all those around me.

I said to Joe, "Which guy? There are a lot of guys there."

He responded, "He's the guy in the grey suit." At just that moment, a guy left the group in front of the display window and seemed to be heading toward the subway.

I made a mental note. I can remember – vividly – feeling like a detective – *All adrenalin* and ready to tail that grey suit to the ends of the earth. We had already decided that I would lead the pursuit, so I quipped, "See ya."

The game was afoot. We walked half a block apart and followed the perp to the subway station. This became a little tricky. There was always a possibility that the half-block distance between the short and the long tail might be ruined because a subway car could come along, ruin our timing and prevent the long tail from tailing the perp and well, I thought to myself, *Should I increase my pace? Should I trot?* No. Trotting is not good, especially since I could swear Mr. Two-Suit had recognized me, or suspected something was wrong.

There are certain rules in sleuthing and the number one rule is "Don't Tip your hand." If anybody suspects they're being followed, it will blow the tail and cover of the private eye. I must admit, I had a kind of hollow feeling when tailing someone. When he or she stops to check out a map, or blow a nose, you just have to go sailing past them, or take out a map, or blow your nose, and hope the long tail picks them up, and then you become the long tail.

Another tough thing to handle was when only three people were on the subway platform; the perp, the short tail and the long tail would all be waiting for a car to arrive. The subway car stops, everyone on the car exits and leaves just the three of us to board. It's kind of hard not to notice each other under those circumstances.

As you can see, there are so many things that can happen while tailing. I can remember following a guy who got off the subway, climbed the stairs and waited for the next subway car going in the direction he had just come from. What to do? l thought I had tipped him off and blown my cover. I decided to take a chance and follow him. Sure enough, when we got to the next stop, he got off and so did I. Suspicious? *Ya* **think?** Needless to say, I moved to the far end of the platform, took the next car and went back to my apartment, where I wrote The Burns Agency my daily report, in which I posed as Mr. Brilliant Surveillant who had just blown his cover!

Now, back to Mr. Two-Suit. We had a very busy afternoon, Mr. Joseph Fallon and Mr. Dave Maynard. We got on two buses, did a little shopping, which included Filene's Department Store, and I wondered whether or not the guy was going to steal some stuff there as well. Then, of all the weird things, the guy went back into Jordan's. I wondered if we had somehow tipped him off as he seemed to sense something was wrong.

Sorry to say, *we* didn't catch him that day, but he was eventually apprehended by a Boston Police officer who went undercover and caught him with the goods.

I must say that the biggest shove that I got from the whole case was a day later when we took up our positions at Jordan's, and when the time came to tail Mr. Two-Suit, Joe crossed the street, walked up to me and said, " It's the wrong guy." We had followed the wrong guy the entire previous day. Well, at least we didn't 'tip' him.

The Night Watchman

As any college student will tell you, if they're smart, one of the best part-time jobs one can have is that of a night watchman. To be truthful, I wasn't too happy when I was instructed by the higher-ups that they wanted me to do such an assignment. After all, I thought, I'm a junior in college and there must be something more they could do with my talents. . . . Ho. ho, ho.

I was informed that, although it might come as a shock to me, in past dealings with college students, they (The William J. Burns International Detective Agency) found that when they placed college students on this kind of job, the students experienced higher grades because they studied harder and more often. In addition, I realized after a short time on the job, that I could toss another wrinkle into it, and that was . . . sleep. Oh how fiendishly clever was I, who worked himself into an enviable position, being paid to sleep. If you wish to emulate my cleverness, take a single bedspread and wrap it around your waist with a belt, wear a loose-fitting jacket which will disguise the fact that you are wearing your night's bedding to work. Oh, one thing; bring an alarm clock. I don't know how other companies handled sleeping on the job, but I simply set the alarm in direct accordance with the company policy. Every three or four hours according to the directive, I would wake up, call in, reset the alarm, and go back to sleep, etc., etc., and I had it down to a science.

By the way, all this snoozing was done in a totally new section of a building which was to become a new wing of Jordan Marsh in Boston. As to my grades, I'm very happy to report an increase of at least half a mark in every subject, except one, and that was economics. That mark increased by a full letter grade.

There was only one mishap, but it didn't make a difference, and that was eating too many nonpareils from the unlocked candy department. I ate them until I was sick. I could barely belt my bedspread when I left work.

Oh, I'd like to relate one more case of wrongdoing, I was assigned to investigate by The William J. Burns International Detective Agency.

By the way, perhaps before I go into my final example of why crime doesn't pay, I should tell you how a case should be handled, how each client was handled.

It's actually very simple. First, gather as much information as possible from the client. Next is the undercover work, and then comes the part I hated . . . confrontation of the perpetrator.

Before I became a sleuth for The Burns–Agency, I thought that all detective agencies accumulated a dossier of evidence. However, it was a little more complicated than that. It turns out they would either try to catch the perp in the act, or compile evidence of wrongdoing, confront the perp with it, threaten to call in the authorities, present the perp with documents they must sign releasing management from all liability related to the case (or words to that effect), and finally a dishonorable discharge of the offending employee.

The Orange Caper

My last story, is that of Hazel. According to the information I was given, she was an employee of New Rochelle Hospital in New York. She was a maid, cleaning women, food server and house-keeper. But most importantly, she was a good listener and would spend her break time visiting with the lonely patients at the hospital. Certain hospital officials rebuked her because it seemed she had a habit of taking oranges from the food trays as she cleared them from the rooms of patients. This, by the way, was during WW II, and fruit was scarce. She reasoned, I guess, that if the patients didn't eat their orange, there was no harm in taking them home to her family.

I observed her and saw two oranges on trays go into the kitchen, and I followed them. I saw her reach for the oranges and said, "Hazel, don't do that. Put it back."

She asked, "Why? Are you going to arrest me?"

I said, "No, of course I'm not going to arrest you, but you must never take anything ever again."

I wrote my report to The Burns Detective Agency, and told them I thought this was much ado about nothing . . . end of report.

I headed home and a little later my mother came in from work. My mother was a nurse who also worked at New Rochelle Hospital where I had just spent the day.

As she walked in, she placed her purse on the kitchen table and said, "How'd your day go, Dave?"

I was about to tell her when her purse tipped over and out rolled . . . three oranges. **No comment!**

Chapter 2

My BIG Break

As a fresh graduate of Emerson College, I walked into the audition room at Boston University. You think you're the only one whose nervous system can be beaten to pieces? Well, nothing was further from the truth. I estimate that there were some 200 people, all of whom seemed to be better looking, better voiced and more confident than me. I had the instant urge to turn and run, but I knew if I did, when I came home, my wife wouldn't let me in the house. And so, I just followed the crowd, took a number from a box, and got back into the line.

Within minutes, rumors were circulating that they were looking for a disc jockey; . . . no, no, they're looking for a newsman; . . . no, no, they're looking for an ace sportscaster; . . . they wanted someone who would work cheap, and it seemed to me that was the last thing I should concern myself with. Salary? *Hell*, get the job!

How well I remember Bill. He had without a doubt, the best voice of anyone there that afternoon. "How was it?" I inquired.

"A snap," he said, "but it didn't make any difference because the money they were going to pay to whomever they hire, wouldn't keep me in a pack of cigarettes." (The average price of a pack of cigarettes in 1952 was about 28 cents.)

Undeterred, I walked into the audition studio and kept thinking, *a pack of cigarettes? . . . I'll give up smoking.*

I got my real surprise of the day when they asked me to do a mock radio show. I said, "What kind of radio show?"

They said, "A disc jockey show."

I said, "I don't have any records."

They told me, "Make them up."

I did a great show, played 10 of the top tunes in Boston and hit with some funny lines, not too many and, just as I was feeling pretty good about myself, the station owner said, "Final auditions are next weekend on Saturday."

My head slumped. It sounded to me like a brush-off.

I remember well waking up that following Saturday. I didn't want to get out of bed.

Then my wife said, "Aren't you gonna get out of bed? Those final auditions are just an hour from now, and we have to drive to the studio."

So I told her, "This is a waste of time. They've probably already picked who they want. I'll be like a bump on a log."

Off we went on our mission of mercy. I want to tell you something. When I was called into the audition studio again, I was a little dismayed – the original three interviewers had become five. They made the request that I do my radio show again. I led off with Tommy Dorsey's *Boogie Woogie* and followed with Patti Page and Tony Bennett. Oh, I was hot now: The Four Lads, Nat King Cole and me. That's right; I was on fire.

A voice over the intercom said, "Come here Dave, will you?" As I stepped into the studio, the astounding words were spoken. "The job is yours. The Dave Maynard Show starts tomorrow at 10 a.m. to noon. You'll also do an afternoon show from 2 to 4 p.m."

Boy, what a dream. Two of my own radio shows and freedom to do whatever I wanted on the air, plus $32.67 take home . . . just enough so I could starve to death! I didn't feel badly because the important thing was, it wasn't pay for delivering newspapers or selling hamburgers. It was for my field of endeavor . . . broadcasting.

What did crafty ole Dave do to supplement his income? I got a second job driving a Checker Cab. I didn't know too much about cab driving, but I did know the best way to talk to the passengers in my cab. I talked them into listening to WHIL and tune in to my shows. I dedicated records, sang *Happy Birthdays* and did everything I could think of to steal listeners from other radio stations.

Yippee! Our ratings started to inch upward, and I got a $5 raise. It was nice eating food again.

Chapter 3

Beantown and Beyond

There are many memorable stories from my radio shows on WBZ. My employment started with them in 1958. When I was hired by 'BZ, I got a big jump in salary to $225. per week. I was by then supporting a wife and three great kids with three more to come.

Playing With the Boston Celtics - 1961

I was put up to play for the station in a charity event to help raise dollars for The Boston Children's Hospital. I didn't get selected because I had a sharp way with the basketball, but because I was 6'1". I was determined to give it my best shot. I was gritty.

I think this would be a good time to mention a player who was definitely an asset to the Boston Celtics, but was almost obscured by the great players who were also on their squad. That fellow was (fanfare, please) Gene Conley (right, in both major league uniforms). Gene was a native Oklahoman and measured 6'8". He served as a

strong rebounder and averaged 6.3 rebounds with an average of 16.5 minutes of playing time per game.

Remember him? He was both a pitcher for the Boston Red Sox, and also a forward for the Boston Celtics; quite the achievement. He was part of the World Series-winning team with Hank Aaron with the Milwaukee Braves, and won three NBA titles in 1959, 1960 and 1961 with the Celtics. That team had Bob Cousy, often referred to as "The Houdini of the Hardwood," as point guard, and Bill Russell at center, a duo know as "Cornerstones of the Celtics."

My job was to guard Gene Conley in that exhibition game. The son-of-a-bitch Conley put me out of the game. We went up after a rebound and I caught the ball first. On the way down, he hit me with his hip. I ended up sprawled on the floor, black-and-blue all over, and under my breath, I muttered a few choice words and, what the hell, even shed a few tears as well. I couldn't play anymore. No question, he was playing to win; a very competitive guy but, for Christ sake, he was playing with Joe Stupid here.

I was nearly killed by Gene Conley. . . . Spread . . . It . . . Around.

Still, there were some perks in playing that game. Years later, as you will see, I was offered a contract with the Boston Celtics. It took about 29 years to snag it though. I'm reproducing it here along with the press release issued by the club.

BOSTON CELTICS

PRESS RELEASE
FOR IMMEDIATE RELEASE
AUGUST 1, 1990

MAYNARD INKS PACT WITH CELTICS

BOSTON…THE **BOSTON CELTICS** HAVE JUST SIGNED
SENSATIONAL CENTER **DAVE MAYNARD** TO A 3-YEAR,
$5,000,000 CONTRACT. MAYNARD, A SLAM-DUNKING, SHOT-
BLOCKING, FLOOR-RUNNING FORCE, SHOULD MADE AN
IMMEDIATE CONTRIBUTION TO THE CELTICS' FAST BREAK.
MAYNARD'S AGENT, **M.L. CARR**, ENGINEERED THIS FANTASTIC
DEAL WHICH WOULD BE ONLY A FANTASY FOR THE AVERAGE
NBA PLAYER. A SPOKESPERSON FOR THE CLUB SAID TO
REPORTERS, "I CAN'T THINK OF ANYONE I WOULD RATHER
HAVE ON MY TEAM THAN DAVE. HE'S THE MOST VERSATILE
BALLPLAYER I'VE EVER SEEN!" MAYNARD BLOCKS MORE
SHOTS THAN MARK EATON AND AKEEM COMBINED, AND HE
RUNS THE FLOOR BETTER THAN ANY OTHER CENTER IN THE
LEAGUE!

And the contract read as follows:

NATIONAL BASKETBALL ASSOCIATION

UNIFORM PLAYER CONTRACT

THIS AGREEMENT made August 20, 1990 by and between the **BOSTON
CELTICS** (hereinafter called the "Association" and **DAVE MAYNARD**
whose address is shown below (hereinafter called the "Player"), In
consideration of the mutual promises hereinafter contained, the parties
hereto promise and agree as follows:
1. The Club hereby employs the Player as a skilled basketball player fir a
term of **3 Year(s)** from the date above. The Player's employment during any
year covered by this contract shall include attendance at any training camp,
playing the games scheduled for the Club's team during any scheduled
season of the Association, playing all exhibition games scheduled by the
Club during and prior to any scheduled season, playing (if invited to
participate) in any of the Association's All-Star Games and attending every
event (including but not limited to, the All-Star Game show and banquet)
conducted in association with such All-Star Games, and playing the play-off
games subsequent to any schedule season. Players other than rookies will
not be required to attend training camp earlier than 4 p.m. (local time) on the
twenty-ninth day prior to the first game of any of the Association's
scheduled seasons.
2. The Club agrees to pay the Player a yearly salary of **$5,000,000** (less all
amounts required to be withheld by federal, state and local authorities, and
exclusive of any amount(s) which the Player shall be entitled to receive from
the Player Play-off Pool). Unless otherwise provided, such compensation
shall be paid in twelve equal semi-monthly payments beginning with the
first of said payments on November 15th of each season above described
and continuing the the first and fifteenth of each month.
3. The Club agrees to pay all proper and necessary expenses of the Player,
including the reasonable board and lodging expenses of the Player while
playing for the Club "on the road" and during the training camp period if the

Player is not then living at home. The Player, while "on the road" (and during the training camp period only if the Club does not pay for meals directly), shall be paid a meal expense allowance as set forth in the Collective Bargaining Agreement currently in effect between the Association and the National Basketball Players Association (hereinafter "the NBA/NBPA Collective Bargaining Agreement").

4. The Player agrees to observe and comply with all requirements of the Club respecting conduct of its team and its players, at all times whether on or off the playing floor. The Club may, from time to time during the continuance of this contract, establish reasonable ruled for the government of its players "at home" and "on the road". Subject to the provisions of the NBA/NBPA Collective Bargaining Agreement, such rules shall be part of the this contract as fully as if herein written and shall be binding upon the player.

5. The Player agrees (a) to report at the time and place fixed by the club in good physical condition; (b) to keep himself throughout each season in good physical condition; (c) to give his best services, as well as his loyalty to the Club, and to play basketball only for the Club and its assignees; (d) to be neatly and fully attired in public and always to conduct himself on and off the court according to the highest standards of honesty, morality, fair play and sportsmanship; and (e) not to do anything which is detrimental to the best interests of the club or of the Association.

6.(a) If the Player, in the judgement of the club's physician, is not in good physical condition at the date of his first scheduled game for the Club, or if, at the beginning of or during any season, he fails to remain in good physical condition (unless such condition results directly from an injury sustained by the Player as a direct result of participating in any basketball practice or game played for the Club during such season), so as to render the Player, in the judgement of the Club's physician, unfit to play skilled basketball, the Club shall have the right to suspend such Player until such time as, in the judgement of the Club's physician, the Player is in sufficiently good physical condition to play skilled basketball. In the event of such suspension, the annual sum payable to the Player for any seaswon during such suspension shall be reduced in the same proportion as the length of the period during which, in the judgement of the Club's physician, the Player is unfit to play skilled basketball, bears to the length of such season.

EXAMINE THIS CONTRACT CAREFULLY BEFORE SIGNING IT.

IN WITNESS WHEREOF the player has hereunto signed his name and the Club has caused this contact to be executed by its duly authorized officer.

WITNESSES:

_____   BY _Arnold "Red" Auerbach_
                                  TITLE

_____   _____
                                  PLAYER
                                  PLAYER'S
                                  ADRESS_____

As you can see I didn't sign the contract with the Celtics. *I felt the offer was too low.*

Community Auditions

Live Telecast Highlights 1965 - 1986

Community Auditions was, to my knowledge, the longest running program that showcased local talent anywhere in the United States. It started in 1950, and was produced at WBZ. Who'd have thought that an amateur talent show, telecast at 11 a.m. on Sunday mornings, would have become a ratings winner for just over 40 years. I don't know whose idea it was to put three judges in the same studio with the amateur talent, but that was done away with by the time the show started. People who are nervous to start with don't need the added pressure.

For those who've never seen the show, let me recall some of the things that happened on Sunday mornings.

First of all, we started with our theme song, which everybody, and, I mean everybody knew. . . .

"Star of the Day, who will it be? Your vote may hold the key. It's up to you, tell us who, will be Star of the Day."

Even now years later, people approach me at grocery stores, at gas stations, at airports, and either start humming that theme song, or they say "Remember me?"

Most times I have to say "No. What year were you on?" My mind goes haywire, so many memories.

Jumping ahead for just a moment: The year was 1997 and we were on a cruise to Central America. The Panama Canal was pretty impressive, but I must admit that when I think of the trip, my mind rivets on Guatemala. After docking, my wife and I grabbed a shuttle bus to Guatemala City for a tour. I was a little dismayed upon our return to find out that while we were touring the city, a U.S. Destroyer had docked next to our ship and had offered a guided tour to everyone on our cruise, but that the opportunity for the tour was over before our return. Well, we walked over to the ship anyway, to take a look. I said to the young Lieutenant who was posted at the gangway, "Is it too late for a tour?"

The officer said, "Hell no. Come aboard."

I told him, "This is very nice of you,"

He said, "Thank you, and by the way, I'm from Melrose, Mass."

After the tour, I was very flattered. As I walked back to the cruise ship, I could hear some kind of commotion behind me, and I don't mind telling you, I was pretty puffed up. The noise was from a Lieutenant Commander on the destroyer, and I waited until he could catch up with us. I said, "Are you from Massachusetts, too?"

"Oh, better than that," he said, "Watch this," and he started to tap dance to the Star of the Day theme song.

In the over-25-years I hosted the show, I tucked away enough memories to last a lifetime. I'll run through a few.

Let me first tell you how the show was produced. Five contestants were chosen from our talent pool. Let's take Frank for instance; he was 11 or 12 years old, and had a pretty nifty little magic act. He had his own tuxedo; what more could you ask for? I sensed that there was something he could add to his act, and so I told him, "Get a white bird."

"A bird?" he said.

"A bird," said I.

Frank said, "Thank you so much!" and out of the studio he dashed.

We tape on Sundays so I kind of doubted he'd be able to do his act incorporating the bird, right away. I was wrong. I got a phone call from him midweek and, I must admit, I was shocked, pleasantly so, when he walked into the studio with a cocker spaniel. Of course, you know, I'm only fooling, as he had a beautiful white dove, just the kind I was thinking of. He had borrowed it from his magician friend, and needless to say, he had to return it when the show was over.

Do you have any idea how much a white dove costs? I haven't given it much thought because I always choke up when I think about it.

Frank was the last of the five acts on the show, and as he was unfolding his card trick in the wings, there were two tap dancers, a baton twirler, and an eight year old boy singer who was to perform the song, "The Impossible Dream."

It's amazing, as you go through life, what sticks to your memory.

The boy, by the way, did a pretty good job singing, but keep in mind he was only an eight year old, doing a song that should have been reserved for an older man. You might ask now, "Why did you have the boy do that song?" Very simple. His mother insisted on it, and you know how mothers are.

Dave with producer Ruth Clennot

Well anyhow, back to Frank the magician. He was the last act on the show and the big dove finale was close at hand. It was pretty tense in the studio. I was nervous; the producer, Ruth Clenott, was nervous; the audience was nervous, because the audience had been at the rehearsal and knew what to expect; but not Frank. It was his finale and with one sweep of his arm and a tiny puff of smoke, the bird appeared and up he went, flying as free as a bird. It went so smoothly that Frank stayed for an extra round of applause, and he got it. We then sang the theme song for the last 20 seconds, and invited the viewing audience to tune in next week for more great talent.

The show was over and nobody moved, except the bird. We could see it up in the rafters of the studio, flying around, but not coming back. This all took place about 20 years ago, and for all I know, the bird is still up there.

Now let's hear about the *Harmonica Hobos* from Hudson, MA. There were 25 boys, ages 9 through 12 singing and playing *I'm Looking Over A Four Leaf Clover*, and they were the show opener. As I watched them go through their rehearsal, I thought, *perfect, well known song, great tempo, good rhythm, winning smiles*, and then they played the harmonicas to an exciting finish. Everybody was happy with it. As we got ready for air time, the Dads were just finishing erecting the bleacher seats for the Hobos, and were down to 30 seconds, the boys were all in position. I'm standing out in front of the group with then 15 seconds to airtime. In a split second, one of the boys cried out, "I'm gonna throw up!"

What happened then? you ask. I'll tell you what happened then. I nearly fainted. I went around and picked the boy up and handed him, just like a sack of meal, to Ruth, the producer. The kids were belting out *Four Leaf Clover* with occasional darting glances at the boy, who was really sick to his stomach, and really throwing up, and really trying to sing at the same time. That boy didn't stop heaving until the show was over and the theme song had been sung.

He was the hero of the day, and rightly so. Guess what? That young boy insisted on singing the theme song again with his fellow troupers. I could have sworn that he kind of inched away from his fellow singers, probably a case of "safety first" on his part.

Now here comes the story of Paul. Actually, I'm not quite sure of his name, but that will do for now. Whoops! I forgot the female member of the group, an enticing, lovely-to-look-at, stunning blonde, eager to be out on the dance floor, doing what I think dance instructors call an Apache Dance. She was four years old. Paul was eight. Let's talk about their costumes. They wore leotards, striped horizontally, kerchiefs tied around their necks, and were barefoot.

The first thing Paul did was to spin his sister across the floor and see how fast he could get her going. Then he would spin her all the way across the floor on her belly. She would tuck her legs up so as to not slow the spin down. Then she started to move to the opposite side of the floor where he was dancing.

Picture this: When she got to the other side, she put herself in a position that we all know and love. When you were a kid fooling around with big kids, or your parents, you would squat a little bit, turn your back and put your hands through your legs so that when you join hands, your partner pulls up from the top. And you end up performing a midair flip.

The stage was set. Paul was dancing around and little sister was in that squat, hands through her legs. Paul danced right past her. Sister dear peered around her legs and said some short quote,

"Paul, Come on!" She didn't say it loud enough because Paul once again danced right past her with a dazzling smile. He didn't realize that his sister was quite a sight.

Ruth and I had been waving like mad to gain his attention. Pretty soon all the members of the audience were waving as well. Now remember, she is still in a bent-over posture and Paul is still dancing around. All of a sudden, he realized he had forgotten his sister. Eight-year-old Paul danced right up to the ballroom veteran, his four year old sister, still in her locked position who was, by this time, pretty steamed. He reached down, grabbed her hands, pulled up and flipped her. She *said* nothing. It was what she did that made the impression on all of us. She slugged him! Not a pitty-pat or a slap, but a knockout blow. He never lost his composure. I saw a woman give him a big hug when the show was over. I could have guessed it was probably his dance teacher, or his Mom.

In the course of 40 years, we often did, "theme shows." We did firefighter shows, police shows, country and western shows, jazz shows; I could go on at great length.

Some of the best shows, talentwise, were the tap dance shows, and I would say, at least 10 girls graduated from Community Auditions to the Rockettes in New York City. I must admit it was torture at Christmas time to spot familiar faces in the Rockettes' lineup as they performed around the country.

Then there was Elliot, an older gentlemen who came in with some auditioning talent, off the street, and came to me with a great idea.

He said, "How about a show that features a group of people who are all 80 or over?"

I said to him, "Why 80? Why not 90?"

He said, "No, a little too old."

I said, "80 doesn't exactly put you in the spring chicken category, but okay, we'll do it."

Eight weeks later, we were all singing the theme song. We had one guy, who blew the hell out of a trumpet, and we had a husband and wife team who were great ballroom dancers, and we had a beautiful lady who sang, *Our Love Is Here to Stay*.

Just before the show started, Ruth took me aside and said, "During the interview with her," (which is part of the show), "ask her to open her left hand and give you a peek inside."

I, of course, asked her on stage, and there they were, three words written on a little piece of paper: "It's Very Clear."

Take a second to ponder it. . . . Have you guessed? It was the first three words of the Ira Gershwin tune, *Our Love Is Here to Stay*. "Just in case fear clutches you," she explained. "Sometimes when I go to sing, I open my mouth, and nothing comes out, so I keep the first three words on a piece of paper in my left hand." By the way, she didn't need the lyric note and she sang beautifully.

It was 1980 when he walked out onto the performing stage, and I had a funny feeling. I'd had the feeling before, and each time I did, it was because I was listening to a super talent. I said to Ruth, "How come you didn't tell me about him?"

She replied, "Just a little surprise I cooked up. You ain't heard nothing yet!"

By the way, he was nine years old. What a waste of nine years. He should have started singing at one!

And there he stood, belting out *I Believe*. He hit every note with power, poise and passion. He had bright red hair, just the right amount of freckles, and after me, one of the most polite persons you could have ever met.

He was a weekly winner on Community Auditions, the Regional Award Winner, and then The Grand Champion for the year!

Dave (far left) with nine-year-old Scotty Grimes (far right) with the performers from that week's show. Right: Grimes today.

No one was surprised be-cause everyone knew that Scotty Grimes was going to be a star. Within months, he was on his way to Hollywood, and within a couple of months, he landed his first audition and appeared in an episode of the *Twilight Zone* called "Little Boy Lost," and on a Bob Hope TV special before the King and Queen of Sweden. Since then, he has had 16 starring roles in movies and TV, so it's safe to say he's going to go a long way.

(Editor's note: Dave was correct. Scotty, now known as Scott, has appeared with such luminaries as The Carpenters and Merv Griffin, and had a role on ER. He appears regularly on TV, in movies, and does voice-over work, all while continuing his music career.)

Ringling Brothers & Barnum and Bailey Circus

Auguste Clown - 1970

The Circus would come in through the railroad station with the elephants. You can't tell now, but those were the good old days, and somehow that is something that can't be done now because it is considered dangerous for some reason, and has gone out of style and that's really too bad.

It was 1970 and I was at WBZ and volunteered to ride an elephant in the parade. I rode an elephant from Copley Square to Washington St. There were lots of people on the sidewalks. I was nearly prickled to death. Those little shoots of hair came up like razor blades. Boy, he could have used a shave!

I went to the Circus and they asked me if I would like to be part of the Walk-About with the clowns. They made me an offer I couldn't turn down. I jumped at the chance, and said, "yes!" They had a midget clown, very nice guy who worked two hours on me with makeup and costume, and made me an "Auguste Clown." I wasn't a tramp clown; that was Emmett Kelley. I wasn't a ballet dancer clown, nor was I an acrobatic clown. There were at least 20 to 30 people in the clown Walk-About.

There is a protocol with clowning around, and no one got to do this unless they got permission from the head clown, Lou Jacobi, and we did. I was dressed up in this outfit with the big shoes and the big red smile. I was given the flower that squirts water, and boy did I have fun with that. I would walk up to the first row of the audience and squirt them, and that alone made it worth doing, believe me.

One of the clowns came over to me and said, "Your son, Matthew, is here with his sister, Megan, and your wife." He said, "Look across from us, about four rows up", and there they were, looking back at us. I had two clowns in back of me, and they had handed me a pie. He said, "Do you want to do this?" and I said, "Don't you worry about a thing."

I couldn't talk because people would get wise to who I was, so, I whistled and gestured for my son to come closer. He stepped forward and I said, "You're some clown, you are!" I put that pie right in the middle of his face.

Then he said, "Dad!"

And I said, "Well, that's how it goes in the big wonderful circus."

Then, to my surprise, as I turned to leave, another clown had sneaked up behind me and I got a pie right in the kisser as well.

Home Run at Fenway Park - 1977

It was 1977 and ten radio stations were invited to send one of their announcing talents to hit a home run at Fenway Park for charity. The program manager at 'BZ asked me if I "wanted to go and hit a home run at Fenway Park."

And I said, "Sure." It was an historic occasion, mildly historic. Each guy would get ten swings. If you hit a home run, there was a pretty good sized cash prize that would go to any chari-ty that we had chosen.

So we all got suited up, and were photo-graphed like we were big time players coming out of the dugout with a bat in hand." All of us felt pretty strutty.

Lee Stang pitched to me and I gave the ball a few good hits, and then I hit one that stopped 6 to 10 inches short of the top of the Green Monster. I cried bitter tears, but if you don't get it to the top, you don't get it to the top! Yes, I ALMOST hit a home run at Fenway Park.

No one got a home run, but they gave the money to charity anyway.

The Arctic Circle

An Eskimo Thanksgiving

I started my all-night show on WBZ radio and took phone calls from the hundreds of thousands of listeners; listeners from 38 states. I say 38 states because my station, WBZ in Boston, was as powerful as any other radio station on the air during the day, but at night, it was gangbusters. In 1978, we were one of only 14 radio stations in the nation to broadcast at 50,000 watts.

In an attempt to show our sponsors what a powerful signal we had, we received phone calls from as far west as San Francisco, California, as far north as the town of Skingatakok in the Arctic Circle, and as far south as Louisiana. To reach these faraway places took excellent weather, and it still was only achieved by the latest advances in transmission equipment.

Well, let's get back to my call from Skingatakok. He called me one November night about 3 a.m. He gave me his name – Joe. Then I said, "You sound like you're calling from pretty far away."

He said, "I am. I'm calling from Skingatakok, up here in the Arctic Circle."

I said, "I thought only Eskimos lived up there!"

He said, "I'm an Eskimo."

Well, my first Eskimo caller. What would I ask an Eskimo? Some thoughts streaked through my mind: *How's Tricks? Do you own a kayak? Do you live in an igloo?* I finally asked him, "Hey Joe, what is the most popular dish in the Arctic circle?"

He answered, "The most popular foods we have are whale blubber and seal meat; easy to keep because everything is frozen."

I said, "Do you fry it, broil it, or roast it?"

He replied, "No, we usually eat it just the way it is."

I asked, "Frozen?"

"Yup," he said.

Then I said to him, "Joe, don't you splurge every once in a while?"

"What's splurge?" he wanted to know.

"You know," I said, "have something special."

"Like what?"

"Well," I said, "in about two weeks, millions of Americans will sit down at the family table and celebrate the Thanksgiving holiday with a big special meal. They will have a roast turkey with bread stuffing, cranberry sauce, root vegetables, pie and cake. Have you ever tasted any of those things?"

Joe said, "No, I haven't tasted any of those things, but I'm going to."

I then asked, "When are you gonna do that?"

And he said, "Our village has a small town hall, and we are going to gather there and eat only American food, all of which you just mentioned. Our government is sponsoring the entire meal."

I said, "I'll bet you're really looking forward to it!"

I could just feel Joe shrug, as he responded. "Well . . . yah," he seemed to say without the slightest bit of enthusiasm.

I thought to myself, *Wait until he gets that first taste of turkey, gravy and a slab of hot apple pie. He'll be a new man.*

I made arrangements to call him back two weeks later, on Thanksgiving Day. My Pilgrim Eskimo answered and said, "Hello."

I said, "Hi Joe. This is Dave Maynard. How's it going?"

He said, "How's what going?"

"You know," I said, "Thanksgiving, the turkey and all the fixins."

He said, "That was good, a little different."

I asked, "How did the meal stack up against your usual diet of frozen whale blubber and frozen seal meat?"

He replied, "I still like my whale blubber and seal meat. A couple of people burned their mouths on the food."

I asked him, "Are you ever going to eat a Thanksgiving meal again?"

Joe responded, "No, I don't think so, but maybe next Thanksgiving . . . if it's free."

Blizzard of '78

"Did someone say, "a little snow?"

It was to become the Blizzard of 1978, but what did I know? I was doing the 10 a.m. to 2 p.m. show on the radio. At that time, I lived in Buzzards Bay, and I just had a funny feeling. They had predicted a snowfall and I knew the drive to the station is a hell of a haul in the snow. I had done it many times. I thought, *Well what could it hurt? I've got a station wagon for goodness sake.* I put another shirt, tie and jacket in the back, and left Buzzards Bay around 8 a.m. on Monday morning, to go to WBZ. It started snowing Monday afternoon. One guy couldn't make his show because he lived in New Hampshire. So we met with the program manager, and those of us on the announcing staff just chopped our time up into two-hour segments, with each guy taking the last guy's place, and the next guy taking his place, and that seemed to work pretty well.

Painting of Marblehead
by Suzan Franks

But I also had to record a television show, Community Auditions, taped between 2 and 5 p.m., and we had the whole audience and talent in studio before it got really bad. Success!

I don't know what we would have done with everyone if they had had to stay overnight, but they were able to get out before the snow got too bad. Thank God. The station put the working staff up at the hotel next door.

I was walking from the hotel to WBZ and I saw someone approaching me. It was Bob Lobel, the sports announcer for BZ, and he said: "Are you ready for your two hours?"

And I said "Yeah." Then I said to him, "Jesus, you look hand-some. Who dresses you?"

Bob said, "You do! These are all your clothes."

And I said, "I thought they looked familiar."

I remember the next day very well. Joe Green, the station's pilot/traffic reporter, was walking down the corridor of the station and asked me if I wanted to go up with him in the helicopter to see what it looked like from the air, and I said, "I sure do!"

We went for the ride up, and it was something. You had to guess where the places were because of all the snow. We were up there for close to an hour and made several reports, I even did some myself. The snow was so deep that it was hard to figure out where we were, and some neighborhoods were indistinguishable. The snow was so high, at least one story's worth, and most people couldn't recognize their neighborhoods on television.

Don Batting, the WBZ newsman was out driving his VW bug to get more material to report. He went under an overpass at Beach-mont Hill in Revere and, as he followed the road, his car was total-ly buried in a snowdrift and icy water.

There were so many stories of people helping people. One woman called in and said, "I know there is no way you can help me so I just guess I'm looking for a little sympathy."

I said, "You've come to the right place."

"Well," she said. "I'm in Everett and I sure could use some milk."

I said, "We can get you the milk, but how can we get it there?"

The next caller was a fellow from Malden and he said, "I'll bring her the milk."

I asked, "How are you going to get it there?"

"I own a Michigan Loader." He plowed all the way from Malden to Everett to deliver her milk!

Everyone wanted to help somebody else. It was a real thrill to be a part of it!

Working The Night Shift - Saving A Life!

It was June 5, 1979, and I was working the night shift from midnight to 5 a.m. doing a talk show. The subject of this particular show was a book about to be published the following day entitled, *The Courage to Live,* a guide for the depressed and those who might contemplate suicide. My guest was Dr. Ari Kiev from New York, author of the book. We had been on the air about 15 minutes and one of my first callers was an individual who identified himself as a retired police officer who said he had just attempted suicide. Suddenly my show became a crisis hotline. He told us he had just drunk a quart of 100 proof vodka and swallowed about 50 Coumadin pills. He told us he had had a recent heart operation which led him to taking drugs, and the drugs caused him to sleep a good deal of the time. We kept him talking, and I can tell you my heart was in my mouth the whole time. I was so afraid I would run out of things to say.

Thank God I had already read Dr. Kiev's book because, during the next 50 minutes on the phone with the caller, we both used a lot of the techniques described in the book to help him. At the same time, my producer, Ruth Clenott, was on the phone with the MDC, and the Boston Poison Control Center. The Boston Police were in contact with the telephone company trying to trace the call.

He asked if I was keeping him on the line in order to trace his call. I told him I didn't have the facilities to do that at the station. He told us he had seven children. As we coaxed information from him, he told us he had worked in the Lower Basin Division of Boston, before taking a medical retirement from the MDC three years earlier.

That night, 38 states and Canada were listening to a real-life drama. I felt it was like a movie script!

Meanwhile, Ruth had contacted the Reading, Mass., police and Officer Brian Richards stayed on the phone listening to the caller and giving me and Dr. Kiev questions to ask him to help determine his identity. Eventually, we were able to obtain enough information from the caller for the Reading police, working as a team, to determine his identity and residence.

The trace was never completed by the phone company.

Suddenly through the phone, I heard knocking at the door, and heard a police officer say, "Hi Bob."

It was the most reassuring thing I had ever heard. Then the caller said to me in a sarcastic, low tone, "Thanks, Dave."

He seemed disappointed that he had been rescued. I asked the police to make sure that they told him that I didn't trace the call. I was very choked up and started to cry at the end of it all.

We were notified, the next day, that the caller was in satisfactory condition at the Winchester Hospital.

It was one night I will *never* forget!

Traffic Tickets

Taking on the NYC Department of Motor Vehicles - 1981

It was a beautiful New England weekday morning in 1981. I was on the air about an hour when I decided, for one reason or another, to start trouble. As I was running over a couple of things in my mind, the door to the studio opened, and in he walked – an average-looking guy in his 20s, obviously nervous, guided by my secretary and co-producer, Ruth Clenott, of *Maynard in the Morning*. Now, at the studio, we had a couple of rules, which were usually broken when the situation demanded. One of the rules was "no visitors while on the air." I knew at once that something was up. Both of them looked like troublemakers, and it was just what I was looking for.

Ruth said, "I'd like you to meet John Restuccia. He's a firefighter," and she walked out the door.

After John was seated, I asked him his name, where he lived, and what he did for a living, stock questions designed to calm him down and make him feel more at ease on the radio. "John, tell us why you decided to join us today on *Maynard In The Morning*."

He said, "I have a whole bunch of parking tickets that I thought you might find interesting."

"Why so?" said I.

"Because they're not Massachusetts parking tickets."

"Ah. Then where are they from?" asked the King of the Troublemakers.

"New York City, and they total $26,590," said John.

"Why don't you put them in a little envelope and send them back?"

And he said, "I did that, and they sent them right back to me."

I said "I have to make a couple of phone calls. You have some coffee, John, and wait."

I got on the phone and called the Registry of Motor Vehicles department in New York City, and was mildly surprised that I got such great service. I spoke with the Registrar of the DMV and introduced myself, told the Registrar the situation, and, *my goodness*, when he found out we were on the air, his mood and manner changed, which had me puzzled.

He said "This is serious business."

I said, "Do you hear me laughing?"

He said "This is a busy office and we've probably had a glitch in the computer, so just tell everybody to send the tickets back, but they will have to be paid for, and then we can reimburse everyone, later."

"Oh sure." I then told him, "We don't have any glitch in our computer, so we'll just send the tickets back unpaid."

Then Mr. Registrar said, "Those tickets will be sent back, return mail, and you'll notice a difference; a $10 parking ticket will also include a late fee fine of $25."

I said, "We won't pay that either."

He said, "Maybe you won't feel so smart when we meet in New York City Traffic Court."

I said, "You're a warm and wonderful person," and so saying, I hung up. I then turned to John and said, "What do you think?" He had been sitting there the whole time I was on the phone.

He said, "You sure let him have it!"

Then I noticed that all the telephone lines were lit, so I said, "Hang on. Let's see what's going on out there."

It was BEDLAM. Hell was breaking loose, and it was about an inch from jamming the switchboard. I loved it. People from all over New England were complaining that, they, too, had been sent NYC parking tickets. It was ridiculous and then it got even more so.

One caller said he got a $950 ticket from the NYC Highway Dept, for his utility trailer with no engine, that had been parked in Natick, Massachusetts's local Sanitation Department parking lot.

The station had calls until 11 p.m. that night. The callers all had tickets issued by New York City. One guy, by the way, was really ripping. He said, "Dave, if you do anything, I want to be a part of it."

I said, "How much is your ticket for?"

H responded, "$520."

I said to John, who was still sitting there in the studio having a hell of a time, "What made you decide to fight these NYC parking tickets?"

He answered, . . . *dumm-de-dum-dum* . . . "I've never been in New York City!"

"Well, what do we do now?" I said. "Maybe someone listening will have a good idea for us."

After about 20 minutes of taking calls, I got one guy who had a great idea. He said "Is there any way we can attack New York? After all, this is a revolution."

I gave it some thought and this is what we did:

As people kept calling up with ideas, we used some of them. For instance, the Greyhound Bus Company gave us two buses to go to N.Y. Then I started to fill them up. We got a butcher, a baker, and a candlestick maker; all kinds of people; people from many different walks of life. We could have taken a couple thousand people with us. In four to five days, we were ready to go.

We left on a Thursday morning. We were stopped outside of Boston by the State Police. This, of course, was a goodwill gesture. We knew they would never give us a ticket for any reason. Well, . . . murder maybe. The ride was uneventful until we reached about New Haven, then we could hear our sister station, WINS, keeping track of our whereabouts. Oh, I forgot to tell you, the day before we left, I put in my order for a cannon.

By the way, do you know how tough it is to rent a cannon? We had thousands of parking tickets with us, and we stuffed those tickets into the barrel of that cannon. I decided I was going to blast all those tickets out of the cannon on the side lawn of Manhattan's City Hall. The Minutemen of Lexington had followed us down in another bus and when we arrived, struck up the Fife & Drum Band for the passengers as we came off the bus. We sure looked cool in our buckled boots, tri corner hats, knickers and blouses – true patriots. One of the Minutemen told me they were taking up a collection for my bail, should I be arrested.

Ed Koch was the Mayor at the time, and we got word that he wouldn't come out to greet us, but I swear I saw him peek through the curtains at us a couple of times. I had to make an executive decision of what to do so we marched across the street toward New York City Hall. We were met by six of NYC's finest. I said to the officer (we were almost nose to nose), his name was Officer Steiner, "Is this as far as we go?"

He said, with a winning smile, "Yup. I'm afraid so."

I only made one statement and that was, "We didn't pay King George, and we're not gonna pay you." Then with a wave of the hand . . . **KABOOM.** It was glorious. All those tickets, blown to smithereens, in front of a cheering crowd.

You might be interested in knowing that I had arranged for champagne and some fried chicken for both buses. We drove right through downtown New York City in the middle of the 5:30 rush hour, raising hell.

I neglected to mention, there were all kinds of reporters there, and somebody said, "You think they'll cover this?"

And I said, "I don't know, but I imagine our sister station, WINS, will."

Little did I know it was a slow news day. We were the lead story on at least five stations. We found out that over $19 Million in traffic tickets had been issued to Massachusetts motorists. Our story was also featured on NBC, CBS and ABC television. I got a call from my father, who was living in South Florida and he said, "David, did you know, by any chance, that your picture was below the fold on the front page of the New York Times?"

I said, "Dad, I don't know if you can get one, but the morning edition of the Miami Herald has my picture on the top of the front page."

Even as far south as Florida, the story appeared in the papers accompanied by a photo. The Sarasota Herald-Tribune of September 4, 1981, carried this story:

Hear Ye, We Weren't In New York!

In New York City, "Minute Man" Dave Maynard holds lists of alleged parking violations adding up to $26,000 in fines for John Restuccia of Newton, Mass., who says he passed through New York once, on a bus. Maynard was one of the busloads of Bostonians who visited New York's City Hall to correct what they called a revolting situation. Together they had received overdue notices totaling over $70,000 from New York's Parking violations Bureau. The trouble was, most said, they have never set foot – let along four wheels – in the five boroughs.

We won. *Ha, ha.* No jail for Dave, and a good time was had by all, especially John."

The Charles River Cleanup

Wow, what a turnout. - 1981

Boredom. That's right, boredom. It was a Friday morning, the sun was out on Soldiers Field Road, which borders the Charles River in Allston (a neighborhood in the western section of Boston). It looked kind of beautiful except for one thing . . . trash strewn all over. Well, as I sat in my studio at WBZ overlooking all this – *BANG* – I got an idea. Let's clean the place up. I turned on my trusty microphone and let er rip, not knowing if I could get the good souls listening to assist me. Then – *BANG* again – I got another idea.

Idea #1: Have one of the TV time salesmen get 5,000 tickets to all the various movie theaters.

Idea #2: Come up with a chit of some kind that would be given, along with the movie tickets for food (McDonald's called in right away to donate the refreshments).

The rules were simple: Come to the mobile studio on the embankment of the river in Allston, hand in one large trash bag loaded with litter, and receive, tickets to the movies and a voucher for some good food from McDonald's. We started the Charles River Cleanup at 10 a.m. and it ran until 6 p.m., never knowing that I could get a couple of thousand people to clean up the Charles River in a day. The first bags of trash got there at 9:59 a.m. It never crossed my mind to keep track of how many bags of trash we collected, and that seems to be something everyone wants to know. Okay, so I'll make up a number. I'll make it 3,223 bags of refuge.

All I can say is, it was a wonderful day. The response we got could easily be placed into the *Great* column. Everyone was there with their bag of trash and everyone's spirits were really running high. One thing you may get a kick out of; . . . a great percentage of the trash collectors wanted to tell me what they had picked up, and some of them wanted to dump their bags as if they needed to pass inspection. More than a few were miffed when we declined to examine the contents of their bags. It's funny how people were when they handed in their trash bag. They proudly shouted out the name of the city, town or village from whence it came. Now that's chauvinism!

It was amazing when we looked at some of the items brought in. Just about everybody started with the morning's garbage, and then brought other various collectibles including two bicycles, various small appliances, some pieces that I swear, looked antique, objects d'art and a rather unusual item, a piece of old rotting timber, which had obviously been in the water. The young fellow who brought it in, pointed out to me that this was only half of it, because, he explained, "the other half was usable."

I thought, *usable? Usable for what?* As it turned out, that young man had just joined the Peace Corps and soon after found

himself stationed in the far flung Pacific. While he was there, he painted the plank with a scene of a beautiful lagoon, sent it to me and it hangs on my wall today. Along with that gift, he included a letter which explained why the lagoon looked so sleepy.

As he put it, "The lagoon was full of sharks, but," he said, "the big difference here is, they don't eat us . . . we eat them."

What a thrill it was when all the cars started arriving with their bundles. Some would drive in and come to a halt. A driver would clamber out saying something like, "Hey Dave. I got a problem. I can't find enough garbage. How about I donate a nice camera, and you sell it for me?"

"Sure," I said, and we proceeded to spend the last couple of hours establishing the first flea market to raise funds for Children's Hospital Boston, and I had that funny feeling that this was going to be the start of something big. I looked out onto Soldiers Field Road and at all the automobiles. I knew we couldn't miss. Next year, . . . The WBZ Farm Stand. *Watch Out.*

Go With the Flo

Exactly what's ON that frank? - 2001

I got a call on the radio show from a woman who said, "Do you have a copy of the Portland Press Herald from Maine, extolling the magic of a lady named Flo?"

As luck would have it, I did, and I have no doubt that she was known by thousands who knew her because of a very unusual restaurant. Excuse me, make that "an eating place," actually located on Route 1 in Cape Neddick, Maine, about 50 miles south of Portland.

It just so happened that I had to drive to Ogunquit, Maine and, just for the heck of it, I took the newspaper article which had the directions to Flo's. It was lunchtime when I arrived, and I explained who I was when I got there. I proceeded with caution as I stepped inside the board and chicken wire establishment. For a moment, I thought I had come to the wrong place. Tables? – none; chairs? – none. It was a one room restaurant and they sold hot dogs. No hamburgers, no pizzas. Only hot dogs . . . steamed hot dogs. Don't you dare ask for a grilled one, because you'll get a sharp, no fooling around reply: Steamed, wrapped in a piece of white bread with a smear of red sauce.

After a little bit, I couldn't help but notice that Flo's Hot Dog Stand was jammed with customers. Then, talk about the rapid-fire service; it came to me that they were able to handle their customer glut because there were no menus in the place. Everybody knew what they wanted the minute they hit the inside. The regulars would hold up a number of fingers, needless to say, one finger for each hot dog, with or without sauce.

Now I felt it was time for me to eat one of Flo's hot dogs with sauce. It was amazing just how fast I ate that hot dog. As she handed me the hot dog, I introduced myself, wondering if that would make any difference. Not with Flo. She went into a small back room from where all the hot dogs were dispensed and I took the moment to speak with her daughter-in-law, who

Artwork by "Diner Don" Sawyer
802-254-6192
Photo courtesy of the artist

was wrapping the steamed hot dogs. I asked her about her

mother's secret recipe. She wouldn't give it to me and so I then said to her, "Gee, it would really be kind of a kick for me to bring the mobile studio up here to Maine and broadcast interviews with your customers who come from far and wide to eat Flo's hot dogs. Would you mind?"

She responded that Flo would *never* let us bring the mobile studio, so I went and asked Flo myself.

Big shot broadcaster from Boston, I turned on the charm.

"Fat Chance," was her response.

I thought it was time for another dog, and as I was chewing away, a customer who had overheard my conversation with Flo told me in no uncertain terms, that I was to stop talking about Flo's Hot Dog Stand on the radio, because it was making it harder for the regulars to get their dogs and go.

Having been "put in my place by the people that matter," I then asked Flo's daughter-in-law if there was anything else I should know before I left the premises.

She said, "Yes, there is one thing. You have to be a little careful here around 3 p.m. We close at 3 p.m. and my mother puts a chair in front of the door. All the regulars know the door closes at 3 p.m., but if you time it wrong, you'll walk into the screen door and it will slam right in your face."

Now for the best kept secret of all. This secret was made public by the Portland Press Herald. The paper asked Flo what made her hot dog sauce so good. Flo was quoted as saying. "We put a little *spite* in the sauce!" When asked exactly what is spite made of, she told them her secret ingredient . . . she spit in the sauce while she made it.

After this secret ingredient was revealed by the paper, the demand for Flo's hot dogs grew by leaps and bounds, and in fact, grew so large that she had to expand to open a second hot dog stand to accommodate the insatiable appetites of her customers.

I sometimes wonder if Nathan Hanwerker, inventor of Nathan's Famous Franks and the world's largest hot dog purveyor, ever envisioned anything like this.

Chapter 4

Hangin' With The Stars

Over the course of my radio and television career, I had the opportunity to meet and interview thousands of tremendously talented and inspiring people. The ones that I have chosen to share with you in this chapter, are some of the most memorable, and in some cases, the most outrageous. I hope you enjoy reading this chapter as much as I enjoyed writing it.

Louis Armstrong - 1952

It was not a day like any other day. I had gone to work for the news station, WHIL. The day was different because I wanted to be on a station that was trying to run as an equal to already established stations and WHIL was new to the market. After we got the station on the air, I sat back and waited for the first positive call that wanted to buy time on our station. Unfortunately, nobody was out there. No calls came in to book time. I realized I was going to do my first interview on the radio station, when my producer said to me, "Do you know who's in town?"

And I said, "No. Who?"

"You know," he said, "You've got to keep up with this stuff if you're going to do battle with the major stations. It's Louis Armstrong."

Right away, fear clutched my innards. I had the producer make a call and said to him, "Make them think that you are a real time producer and tell them I will put them on first."

What the hell. Not only was this my first interview, but I didn't have any second, third or fourth for that matter.

The phone rang, and it was Louis Armstrong's manager, and he wanted to talk to me. So I was feeling like, *I'm a big time, big shot.* The manager told me that he and Louis had stayed out 'til 7 a.m. and he (Louis) was sound asleep, and he (the manager) dared not wake him, but he said "When he wakes up, I'll give you a call."

I got the call and drove to the Copley Square Hotel, got inside and doffed my coat. Through the whole time, I'm trying to act like Joe Monterrazzo (a noted Boston figure of the time), anybody, but me. They told me to go to the third door and he'd be inside. So I took the microphone and walked over to the door. Louie stepped out halfway. Picture this: here he is about to do an interview with me, I showed up on time, brought all my equipment, including collapsible microphone. I'm ready, and he hadn't done anything. He had on one of those strappy undershirts with a straight razor in his hand. He was shaving.

I said, "Wow, you look cool."

And Louis said, "You look kind of cool, too."

We ended up doing quite a long interview. Louis was doing all the typical facial contortions as he shaved with that straight razor. He would start to talk and his voice would sound funny as he pursed his lips, and I was thinking, "Louis, will you sit up and take notice so you can help me get this interview done." But I didn't.

Then he told me a story of a group of his musicians on a trip from New York to Los Angeles. It's a long trip by train. The train was called the 20th Century, and one of the band members, a trumpet player, was shaving as the train was going through Altoona, Pennsylvania. There was a place the train passed through called the "Big-Ass Curve." Suddenly, the train hit the curve and lurched, shaking from side to side, a very dangerous situation. Almost simultaneously, a blood curdling scream was heard by everyone. Louis's friend and fellow trumpet player had sliced off a piece of his top lip. Goodbye vocation for him. He would never play the trumpet again. He didn't have a choice.

Then Louis said, as he continued shaving with that straight edge razor blade, "That's why we take a little longer in this interview. No sudden moves. I need to be careful with my chops."

Jimmy Durante

Ah, there was a great guy, Jimmy Durante. I interviewed him, as well. Jimmy was a very happy guy, a guy who loved what he did. I was very sorry to hear that in his declining years, about 1989, he took sick with prostate cancer. It is always sorrowful when someone is struck down and has to go to a nursing home. He was always on, always on. Except for the last three years or so, he had a zest for life. I heard from two different sources that he was suffering. He was not bitter, because he was the kind of person that couldn't be bitter, but he was sorrowful. He felt badly, because nobody came to see him. He died lonesome. It was very sad indeed.

Jimmy Durante died on January 29, 1986, in Santa Monica, California, at the age of 86. Just who was Jimmy Durante? Born in 1893, James Francis Durante was a lot of things. He was a singer, a pianist, a comedian, and an actor. His distinctive gravel voice, comical language butchery, his influence on jazz, and let's not forget a large nose, helped make him one of the most familiar and popular personalities from the 1920s through the late 1970s. The jokes about his nose included him referring to it as his *schnozola*.

Jimmy dropped out of school in the eighth grade to become a full-time ragtime pianist.

In his early teens, he joined his first band, *The Original New Orleans Jazz Band*, which he took over in 1920 and changed the name to the *The Jimmy Durante Jazz Band*. Durante became a vaudeville star and radio personality by the mid 1920s and made his first stage appearance in Cole Porter's new musical, *The New Yorkers*, which opened on Broadway in December of 1930.

By 1934, he had his first major record hit with his own composition, *Inka Dinka Do,* and it became his theme song for the rest of his life.

A year later, he starred on Broadway in Billy Rose's production of the stage musical, *Jumbo.*

He made stage history when the show began; the scene opened with Jimmy leading an elephant down an alleyway when a police officer stopped and asked him, "What are you going to do with that elephant?"

In his show stopping reply, Jimmy said, "What elephant?" and brought the house down.

After appearing in three more Broadway productions, he headed to Hollywood, where he began appearing in a comedy series pairing him with silent film legend, Buster Keaton. He appeared in such films as, *The Man Who Came to Dinner*, starring Bette Davis; and *It's a Mad, Mad, Mad, Mad World*. He also appeared on the popular radio program, *The Chase and Sanborn Hour*, which he eventually took over, when the star of the show, Eddie Cantor, left.

Next he teamed with a crew-cut newcomer to American radio whose name was Garry Moore.

The big schnozola made his television debut in November of 1950 in an NBC comedy variety show called, *The Big Show.* How's this for a lineup: comedian Fred Allen; singers Mindy Carson, Frankie Laine, Ethel Merman; Actor Jose Ferrer; and a new comic singer by the name of Danny Thomas.

By August of 1955, *The Jimmy Durante Show* was going full blast on the Vegas Strip. Featured in one of her last performances was the famous Brazilian singer, Carmen Miranda. As they sang and danced together across the floor, Miranda fell to her knees while Durante instinctively told the band to "Stop the Music!"

They stopped and Miranda got on her feet, but whispered to Durante, "I'm out of breath."

"Okay, honey," said Durante, "I'll take your lines."

She laughed and quickly pulled herself together and finished the show. Sadly though, her life ended one day later from heart failure.

What do these songs have in common? *September Song, As Time Goes By, My Foolish Heart, Make Someone Happy*, and quite a few others including, *Inka Dinka Do*, and *Umbriago*? Of course, they are all hits by Jimmy Durante.

My mind goes back many years to when I was a kid of ten, lying on the floor, listening on the radio, and laughing at the antics of Jimmy Durante and Garry Moore. If I had to select the biggest laugh getter from Jimmy, my favorite would be a replay of a short skit that you might catch on the movie channel one of these nights. It went like this:

> A group of people were waiting to get onto an elevator, including a buxom, but agitated, blonde. Suddenly, Jimmy approaches and quickly scoops the blonde up in his arms. Our Prince Valiant Jimmy then asks the stunned buxom blonde which floor she desires, and just as the elevator opens, he strides in with her, she, still captured by his embrace. He then turns to the crowd still waiting for an elevator and shaking his head, and with his most infectious smile says, "Sixth floor please, and don't forget to bring a lot of salami!"

Maybe you had to be there. Everything he said made you laugh. To this day, I don't know what he meant by that salami line, but it *sure* made me laugh.

By the way, I don't know who Mrs. Calabash is, either.

Warren Beatty

I had been plugging him all week, and I was determined to make his acquaintance.

I was doing the mid-morning show in January 1967 on WBZ. One of my children said, "Warren Beatty is going to be at the station and on your show today. Did you know that?"

I said, "Yes, I do know that." Then she asked if I could get her an autograph, and I said, "I'll try."

Warren Beatty is an actor, producer, screenwriter and director and has been nominated for 14 Academy Awards during his career. At the time, he was promoting his latest movie, *Bonnie and Clyde,* and he was to be nominated as Best Actor by The Academy for his role as Clyde, later that year. As you can tell, he was a pretty popular guy.

Warren Beatty was coming to the studio, but I was told when I got to the studio that he wouldn't be able to make my radio show because his managers had overbooked him, and he would only be able to do the television segment.

Well, I thought to myself, here I am just six or seven studios down the corridor, and on the air. He could at least come in and say *hello*. After all, I'd been plugging his appearance for some time, so this was a case of saving face.

There was a back way from the radio studio I was in, to the television studio he was in, so I cooked up a plan. I kept a record in the studio, a song named *McArthur Park*. It ran over seven minutes, and I kept it handy for just these kinds of emergencies.

When someone I wanted to interview was in the television studio, I would slap on that record, zip out the back, and take the shortcut to the television side of the building. So I put on the record, got over to the TV studio, walked in and said, "Where is Warren Beatty?" They told me he was in the men's room.

I said, "Oh my God," and raced to the men's room. I burst in and there were only two people inside; Warren Beatty and me. It was a large room with six to eight sinks on one side, and the urinals on the opposite side. He was at a urinal and I got across the way from him and shinnied myself up on a sink.

I was sitting there and he wasn't reacting, so I started humming a familiar tune. Oh how I remember it well, *Unforgettable, That's What You Are*. He heard that and turned around and said, "What ARE you doing?"

I said, "Well, my kids are going to ask me. Did I see Warren Beatty today, and I can now say, '*Did I see* Warren Beatty!'"

He replied, "You are a sick Son-of-a-Bitch."

Three months later, Shirley MacLaine, Warren Beatty's sister and also a multi-award winning actress, came by the radio station for an interview. I proceeded to tell her the Warren Beatty story. Upon conclusion, she said, "You *are* a sick son-of-a-Bitch!"

I told her, "You people are all alike."

Julia Child

I'm convinced that Julia Child was an operative for the CIA. After all, how many people do you know who could handle information of a military nature and, the recipe for Duck a l'Orange at the same time?

I had a great time from 1980 to 1985. I was doing some cooking segments with the world renowned culinary chef, Julia Child, on the WBZ-TV Evening Magazine with Robin Young. I had interviewed Julia on my radio show many times, and she and I had become friends. I was impressed with Julia because she got there the tough way with the study of culinary arts and dedicated hard work.

Julia was born in August, 1912 and passed away in August, 2004. During her lengthy career, she was seen cooking away on various television shows, and can still be seen on cable and PBS stations. In 1996, Julia Child was ranked number 46 on TV Guide's *50 Greatest TV Stars of All Time,* and during her career, authored 13 cookbooks, some on cassettes, from 1963 with *The French Chef,* to 2000. She ended her last book with the words, "Thinking back on it now reminds me that the pleasures of the table, and of life, are infinite. *Toujours, bon appetit!"*

I'm sure we have all walked into situations where we don't know anyone, but we do well because there's that one person in the room who makes us feel at home, comfortable, and who gives us a lot of confidence. She was that kind of person. She made us feel confident. She WAS, after all, *The French Chef.*

The first time I made an appearance on her show, I was in her kitchen on Irving Street in Cambridge. I felt like I was in the Nazareth of cooking when I came in to do the show. She had every cooking utensil and, every saucepan known to man on the wall and on the ceiling, I said, "You have all this stuff to cook with."

She said, "Of course. I'm a cook."

"But," I reminded her, "not every cook is Julia Child."

The most important thing about presenting yourself on television – a major part of the ingredient – is confidence. That's the most important ingredient, beyond a shadow of a doubt, and she gave that to me as we worked in her kitchen.

So I asked, "What are we going to cook this morning?"

She replied, in her typical scratchy voice, "Well, I thought we would make a little mayonnaise."

I said, "Fine. Sounds great to me," since I knew we have all had a situation where we ran out of mayonnaise and now we were actually going to learn what to do in that emergency.

"It's only eggs and oil and you whip it," she said.

After about five or six takes, I was spellbound and didn't care if it took 100 takes. In the middle of it all, this fellow walks in. Yes, in walks this guy, with a little flamboyance, and totally dislikable. At least he was that day. He said *hello* to some of the people on the set. He spied me, came over and said, "What are *you* doing here?"

I replied, "Whatever that lady is doing," nodding toward Julia.

Then he said, "That lady being my wife?" He then said to Julia, "What are you doing here?" He spoke to her as if she had no business being there on the set . . . in her own kitchen, and I thought to myself, she *IS* the set.

She said, "Mr. Maynard and his crew are here, and his assignment is to interview me, and I thought we would make a little mayonnaise."

He was a little inebriated and, with a harrumph, walked out the door, and she acted like it never happened. No ruffled feathers on her. She was a true professional. We didn't even lose our cadence and continued on.

By the way, the next time we did a segment, I asked her if we could do something entirely different, not something that everybody's done, because that's why she had become such an important person to millions of Americans.

So I said to her, "Let's get Wacky."

She said, "What do you mean by Wacky?"

And I said, "Let's do some dessert."

"Well, to tell you the truth, I was futzing around in the kitchen this morning, and I have a new recipe for everyone to try out." We then made it together. She said, "It starts with vanilla ice cream, then you sprinkle 1 ½ teaspoons of instant coffee on the top, and then end it off with 2 tablespoons of Bourbon." Boy. It was delicious!

As I mentioned, she made me feel totally at ease. So much so, I could have done a show with just myself, without her, because she made me feel that comfortable. I wonder how many people meeting her for the first time had that same feeling. To talk to her for ten minutes was an adventure. You couldn't help but feel as if you'd known her for at least a decade because she just had that way about her.

Picture this; a lady over six feet tall with a unique, high pitched, scratchy voice, and one heck of a disarming personality. In short, she was a charmer, a genuine A-number one hero for so many of us.

It didn't come as a surprise to me when I heard and read that she had been approached by the OSS (Office of Strategic Services), precursor to the now well-known CIA. Are we talking about spying here? Yes, perhaps.

I think it's a good idea that I call your attention to a book authored by Jennet Conant entitled *A Covert Affair*, published in April 2011. Conant recalls the years Julia and her husband, Paul, worked for the OSS. Conant did three years of research and her book says that Julia was *NOT* a spy.

I disagree. Not only do I believe that Julia Child was an operative with the CIA, and a damned good one at that, I expect someone will step forward and make the case that Julia was a double agent. If MI 6's James Bond could do it, there's no doubt in my mind that Julia could as well. After all, how many people do you know who could handle information of a military nature and, the recipe for Duck a l'Orange at the same time?

Could it be the same person who posed for a Valentine's Day card in 1956, nude, with her husband, in a bubble bath, with a heart shaped caption above them that read: "Wish You Were Here. Happy Valentine's Day,"

mailed from Puttersdorf, Germany, and sent to J. Edgar Hoover, then Director of the FBI?

The postcard was sent in response to a recent McCarthyism-type interrogation by the FBI of her husband, Paul, regarding his relationship with a former girlfriend who turned out to be a spy and, to add insult to injury, the interrogators asked him humiliating questions that intimated his masculinity was under suspicion and a target as well. That postcard showed a lot of moxie. That was Julia!

As they say, "The proof is in the pudding," and we all know. *Nobody could do that better than Julia!*

"Fats" Domino

A lot of people emulated his style. He was there at the very beginning of Rock and Roll.

When it comes to music, we need to start with Antoine "Fats" Domino. It's only right to start with him because he started Rock and Roll. I remember well, disc jockeys all over the United States, if they were smart and knew anything about the record industry, would play his records. Unfortunately, some of them weren't so smart, and the one thing they all found out was, you can't stop a hit record!

What was first called rhythm and blues soon became Rock and Roll, and the spearhead jock was Alan Freed of WINS out of New York City. I remember the first rock and roll hit, *I'm In Love Again,* by "Fats" Domino, and the second was probably *Gee,* by the Crows. Within six months, there had to have been at least 200 hits. It was like wildfire. All those disc jockeys who refused to play his records were very quiet. God knows how many station managers went to their music directors with the same queries: "What the Hell is going on here?" and "Why aren't we playing that shit?" I understand that there was a lot of starvation going on for those stations that didn't play his popular songs. Too bad.

I remember the afternoon he was on my show. We had roughly an hour to work with. We really didn't have much to do in that hour. Antoine (his real name), if he had been a bit more gregarious, could have probably done five more interviews in the time allotted to him, and still would have had time to recite the *Gettysburg Address*, The *King's Speech* from *Hamlet*, and *The Wreck of the Hesperus*. In other words, you never have to worry about him schlepping around with the English language. He let his music speak for him.

Some stats on Fats: He was born in 1928 in New Orleans. His first language was French. He first performed on the piano and sang when he was 10 years old. At 14, he left school and had a number of jobs working in factories. He worked days so that he would have the time at night to perform.

He signed his first recording contract in 1949 with The Imperial Record Company, and it didn't take him very long to have a record on the charts for all to see. Nothing could have stopped him and his music . . . nothing.

At his first recording session, he made sure he recorded a Voodoo God good luck song entitled *Hey! La Bas Boogie.* He also recorded a cleaned up version of a song about drugs called *The Fat Man,* which reached number two on the Rhythm and Blues charts in 1950.

Fats burst onto the Rock and Roll scene in 1955 with his song, *Ain't That A Shame.* The song was covered (recorded) by Pat Boone and made it to number one on the charts, with Fats's version coming in at # 10 (but # 1 on the R&B chart). That song established them both as stars. He went on to record the classic *Blueberry Hill,* and other classics like, *I'm Walkin',* which was covered by Ricky Nelson. That song helped launch Ricky's career as well.

In the 1950s, Fats sold over 65 million records, outselling every other rock and roll artist with the exception of Elvis Presley.

He currently lives in New Orleans with his wife Rosemary and is the recipient of the Grammy Lifetime Achievement and Hall of Fame awards. He was invited to the White House in 1998, by then President Clinton, to receive the National Medal of Arts award. However, he had said in 1980 that he would never leave New Orleans again, and this included attending that ceremony.

He didn't attend his induction into The Rock and Roll Hall of Fame in 1986, either. Next time you visit New Orleans, look around, be sharp, and if you see a big roly-poly man with a smile on his face, wailing away on that wonderful piano, *stop, . . . turn,* and walk in. By the way, if you have a chance, thank him for me again, for that beautiful wristwatch he sent me for Christmas some years ago.

Zsa Zsa Gabor

Zsa Zsa's combination of drop dead gorgeous good looks, delightful Hungarian accent and come hither femininity turned every man she met into a pool of putty!

Zsa Zsa was born in Budapest, Hungary and named Sari Gabor. She was the middle child of three between older sister Magda and younger sib, Eva.

Their maternal grandparents chose to remain in Budapest during the war, thinking they had a safe place to hide. Unfortunately, the U.S. bombed Nazi targets near where they were hiding, and both perished.

There's no two ways about it, I don't care if word gets around, but I am a member of the Zsa Zsa Gabor Fan Club. Member? Hell, I'm President At the time of this writing, she is 93 years old and has been in and out of the hospi-tal many times in the past ten years or so. I don't care. I love her just the same and, believe me, when we met for the first time I was prepared to accept the fact that she was, or seemed to be, a foolish loudmouth. She was neither.

She was late getting there, and I was under a terrible time han-dicap. We told her manager she had to get to the station, but he told us that she was running late, and I was ready to do her in, in a nice way of course, but doing her in; that was a definite possibi-lity. All of a sudden the door opened and she swept in. She didn't walk in, she *swept* in, and I thought, *Oh, boy.*

Come to find out, she was very knowledgeable. She was working for a cosmetics firm promoting their latest cosmetic line.

She brought with her a beautiful fitted case, which she opened up and said, "This is for your wife."

It was a gorgeous thing, full of cosmetics. What a nice gesture. We loosened up and did a hell of an interview.

She was much different from what I expected. She struck me as being stunningly beautiful; very, very smart; witty; clever; and with great cleavage as well."

Speaking of cleavage, I remember watching The Johnny Carson Show one night, and he had first interviewed Debbie Reynolds, star of stage and screen, who was wearing her signature 16" pearl necklace. When Zsa Zsa came out, she was wearing two long strings of pearls and Debbie complimented her on how beautiful they were. Zsa Zsa responded, "Oh, darlink. You must get yourself a pair like mine, because when they

Zsa Zsa with her pearls.

drape down on your bosom, it makes them glisten so."

Debbie thanked her for the advice, but wasn't sure if she would be able to achieve the same glistening effect as her friend. The audience roared with laughter.

Zsa Zsa is unique. She's a woman who would have felt at home in the court of Louis XV. Somehow, though, she manages to pull this off while living in the 20th and 21st centuries. She seemed to fit in with the Pompadours and the Du Barrys, but then again she would be quoted as saying, "I always was a goof. I pay all my own bills, and have always chosen the man. I don't permit a man to choose me."

And she has, having married nine times. Now that's choosey. As a matter of fact, because her marital history was part of her charm, I asked her, "Zsa Zsa, how many husbands have you had by now?"

And she responded, "You mean other than my own?"

Talk of Gabor's high number of divorces served two purposes. It gave her plenty of material, and she used it well, with her natural knack of making people laugh. One of her most quotable puns is, "I am a marvelous housekeeper. Every time I leave a man, I keep his house."

Zsa Zsa's combination of drop-dead gorgeous good looks, delightful Hungarian accent and her come-hither femininity turned every man she met into a pool of putty.

However, something must have gone wrong in one instance, because while married to Conrad Hilton (of Hilton Hotel fame), she admitted to having a sexual tryst with her stepson, Nicky Hilton.

Now, if you're saying to yourself, "Is that the same stepson that married Elizabeth Taylor?" the answer is, *Yesirree.*

I always considered Nicky Hilton to be a lightweight, but after all, where the heck do I get off criticizing Nicky. His track record is rather impressive, and is in print constantly, which includes some pretty striking sexual statistics. Maybe he just asks nicely.

I'll say this for Zsa Zsa: after her death, there will be love stories that will make your head spin. Believe Them All! God Bless.

Phyllis Diller

"If I took off everything that isn't me what you'd see is a flat-chested, bald, little old man!" --- Phyllis Diller

Phyllis Diller: Ah, yes. What can you say about a lady who can make you laugh anytime, anyplace? I remember one of my fellow broadcasters, who said to me while passing in the corridor, "Are you gonna have that wacko broad on your show tomorrow?"

AP photo, Kevork Djansezian

"Why?" I asked. "Does she have some kind of rare social disease? How could you tell if she did have one?"

"Man," he said. "She is ugly!"

"You ain't no Warren Beatty yourself," I said. You see, I had seen both her appearances on the Jack Parr Show and she brought the house down, both times.

What was really most important, she had made *me* laugh. Not a snicker, not a big happy smile. Full belly laughter. Then more full belly laughter.

She was here to perform at Fort Devens. It was the era of mini-skirts and when she pranced out on the stage, doing the model's walk, I must admit, I didn't even notice that her legs were just one step ahead of popsicle sticks. Then she said, "Stop the music!" and stared down at the audience for a full 10 seconds, and said, "Look at that" pointing to her spindly legs, "and I'll tell you something else. They don't go all the way up. I am a collection of spare parts that include my fright-wig, legs by Amalgamated Pipe Cleaners and arms by Party Toothpicks. Every morning, I don't get dressed, I get assembled. If I took off everything that isn't me, what you'd see is a flat-chested, bald, little old man.

"Many times I have been called ugly, I'll tell you what ugly is . . . I once found a guy hiding under my bed, and he was my date.

"I'm determined to grow old disgracefully . . . but I need help. Any volunteers?

"I want you to know I *do* have a backup plan. I wear a Medic Alert bracelet that reads, *In case of emergency, please give me extra mouth to mouth.*" She brought down the house . . . again.

I wish I could repeat some of the things she said in the car returning home from the base. It was just the two of us sitting in the back seat. "Be tender to me. After all, I am church people," she said.

I said, "Trust me, trust me."

Then we were off and running. As we were driving through Lexington, Mass., I said, "How about a side trip, Baby?"

"What do you have in mind?"

"Do you like big old houses?"

"How big?"

I said, "nineteen rooms."

She said, "I'd freak out!"

I responded, "I wouldn't want to miss that."

We drove to my house: five-and-a-half bathrooms, six fire-places, nineteen rooms; with a swimming pool and four car garage on one-and-a-half acres, located in one of the most desirable parts of Lexington. It was the kind of house that could turn just about anyone into a snob. Another neat thing was the circular driveway, on which we had some really great touch football weekends.

After the tour, I turned to her as we sped down Route 2 and said, "Well, how'd you like it? Pretty swell, huh?"

"Shut up!" she said. "Don't say another word. I'll have a house like that one day. You'll see." (And in five years, she had divorced her husband, Fang, bought a huge old house in Pacific Palisades, California, and was still hotter than a pistol.)

I asked what she liked best about the house and she said, "That's easy. The bathrooms, and then I would be rid of all those hotel bathrooms. You know, the ones where you practically break a hip every time you try to turn around and reach for the toilet paper."

We soon arrived at her hotel. The manager greeted her with a cheery smile and asked the age old question, "Are you pleased with your accommodations, Ms. Diller?"

And she responded, "Shit!"

Nat King Cole

I remember it like it was yesterday. *SNAP*. I turned on the radio. I was just 15 and listening to the greatness of Nat King Cole.

The year was 1942 or 1943 when I turned on the radio in my spiffy 1937 Ford Roadster. Boy, did I love that car, and I loved it even more because I am a music freak and the tenor of music was changing. It was no longer just big band music. It was pop music. It was being played on radio stations all over the country, practically – one new hit per week. I remember it like it was yesterday. *SNAP*, as I turned on the radio and the mellowest voice I've ever heard, then and now, sang out *Straighten Up And Fly Right*. A goofy

song about a buzzard who takes a monkey for a ride, but it was his delivery that made the song a hit!

The singer was one who became a legend in his own time. He recorded songs like, *Too Young, Embraceable You, The Christmas Song*, and countless others. His songs were slow and melting, and every now and then he would sing about the *Duration Blues*, by Johnny Mercer. How about this for a song concept, the depression and that new thing called Spam (the food, not the internet kind)!

Can you imagine if today somebody wrote a melody and lyrics about shortages due to a war effort? He was the leader of the Nat King Cole Trio. He played sensational piano as well, and sold as many records as anybody in the United States.

I must admit that I became a little frustrated every time we would arrange to meet each other. Something would come up and our schedules would clash. Finally, one night at the Worcester Auditorium, where he was appearing, and I was emceeing, Sherm Feller walked up to me and said, "Have you met Nat?"

I said, "No."

Sherm said, "He would like to meet you, but he had an accident."

And I thought, *Oh, no. Here comes one of those circumstances again.* I said, "What kind of accident was he in?"

Sherm replied, "A waiter spilled a soup bowl full of beef stew on his tuxedo pants."

Even as we spoke, someone was rushing his pants back from a nearby dry cleaners. Talk about aplomb. There in his dressing room, in his top hat, white tie and tails . . . but no pants; good looking shorts though. Naturally, he's my hero and there he stood. *Cool man, cool.*

On one tour, Nat came to perform at Blinstrub's and he brought the whole family with him; Maria, his wife, and the two girls, Cookie and Sweetie. My wife arranged for a babysitter for the girls and we all went to the show. By the way, Sweetie was daughter Natalie's nickname.

I remember very well, with sadness, the regal looking cigarette holder that he used. I

Dave meeting Nat King Cole

thought of it many times, especially when I heard that Nat was diagnosed with inoperable lung cancer. When he toured, he always tried to mix into his schedule, trips to various veterans' hospitals. He would start off by making an announcement by saying, "See this," holding up a lit cigarette, "It's going to be the death of me, and maybe you, too, if you don't stop smoking."

By the way, if you are unaware of the tremendous talent of Nat King Cole, I suggest you take a saunter to your nearest music store and ask for Nat King Cole and his daughter, Natalie's, CD titled, *Unforgettable.* You won't be sorry. If you can't find that, maybe you can get your hands on a copy of *Sweet Lorraine* instead.

The Searchers

"It was a one punch steam fitter knockout!"

This is a short, happy saga. It took place at Canobe Lake Park, one of the finest amusement parks I have ever seen, and how lucky we were to have it, so ideally placed to serve the people of New England, located in Salem, New Hampshire. Anyone who has ever visited there would easily testify it had everything. It was peaceful, yet exciting. You could hear an abundance of laughter, and only one time in the ten years I ran dances in the ballroom, did I hear a harsh word.

It was a Friday night in July and the British Invasion had just started. The Beatles, of course, opened the door for loads of British rock groups. On this night we sponsored the American premier of a group called *The Searchers*. They were also from Liverpool, and certainly showed their British charm. They played pretty good too.

Halfway through the evening, I called for a 30-minute intermission. The band filed out to a little restaurant next door, sat down and ordered hamburgers. They were served promptly, and ate everything quickly, save one band member. Most of them made a semi-hasty retreat back to the ballroom because the kids at the dance were trying to get closer to the band members as they tried to eat.

The band members went back inside; all but the bass player who hadn't finished his hamburger yet. The poor guy was having more of a problem answering all the questions of the attendees, and not getting to finish his meal. Then, for some reason, a handful of admirers, or I thought they were admirers, started to get, I felt, a little too loud. I could just feel trouble brewing, so I suggested to the bass player, "Why don't you finish your hamburger inside."

He said, "That's all right," set the hamburger down and turned to leave. I slipped inside the dance hall to make sure everything was running smoothly. I wasn't inside more than five minutes when I heard sounds of a ruckus, and one or two screams.

I grabbed a cop who was near-by. I beckoned to the bass player to get inside because it was obvious the major instigator was going to try to do bodily harm. At the same time, a troublemaker broke through the crowd and took a swing at the bass player, and connected. The bass player never moved, except to take a swing of his own. He only hit the trouble-maker once, and knocked him out.

I didn't see the swing itself, but there were a lot of people standing around saying, "Wow," or, "Holy Mackerel."

Get this. He hit the punk in his stomach. We had a little pow-wow and I said to the musician, "How come you hit him in the stomach?"

With a wry smile, he said, "It usually works."

Then one of his band mates said, "Tell Dave what you did for a living before you began to play with us."

He told me, "I made my living as a pipe fitter."

I told him I sure hope *I* didn't do anything to offend him.

Bobby Darin

He was a fellow who wanted to sell a million records. It just didn't happen as fast as he wanted.

Walden Robert Perivale Cassoto was born May 14, 1936, in Bronx, New York and died at 37, on December 20, 1973. It's amazing when I look back on it now, that he had so much talent. Most people looked upon him as a rock and roll singer, but he was far more than that. He was a vocalist, a very successful songwriter, guitarist, drummer; everybody who saw him perform in person said he was a knockout harmonica player.

Pop, Rock, Jazz, Folk, Country. He could do it all and surprised a lot of people, including yours truly. Another thing about Bobby Darin was that his health was dangerously fragile and, needless to say, he knew it. He frequently displayed that inner push to succeed as a songwriter, accomplished musician, instrumentalist, whatever. His recording career started in his mid-teens and after recording three or four songs, managed to hit pay dirt with, *Splish Splash*. I remember well, the day that record was released. He got right on an airplane and went on a promotional tour of Boston, New York, Philadelphia, Pittsburg and Cleveland, plus a couple of others. He had a smash and made sure everybody knew it.

Who the hell was Bobby Darin anyway? He was the fellow who was gonna sell a million records. It just didn't happen as fast as he would have liked, because of course, there was always a specter hanging over the horizon. He had a very weak heart, but you'd never know it to look at him.

On his way up the ladder of success, he met, wooed, and married the lovely actress, Sandra Dee (Shown at left). They plunged into filmmaking together in 1961. The film was called, *Come September*, and it was moderately successful. Besides acting, he still churned out a number of songs.

Let's see if I can dig up some familiar titles.

How about: *Rock Island Line, I Found a Million Dollar Baby, Dream Lover, Beyond the Sea, You're the Reason I'm Living, If I Were a Carpenter,* and God know how many more hit sounds.

Of course, never to be forgotten *Mack The Knife* which sold over two million copies in a very short period of time.

His wish for a legacy was to be remembered as "a human being as well as a great performer," and among many of his contributions, he became Good Will Ambassador for The American Heart Association.

For a while, there was an almost-romance budding between a divorced Bobby Darin and a kind of mixed-up Connie Francis. Connie had a very strict and super-protective Italian father who traveled with his daughter around the nightclub circuit. You could catch Connie's father, Harry, counting the house every night she played Blinstrub's Village in South Boston. I know. I saw him. Because Connie was paid by the number in attendance, he didn't want to get cheated, and so he did that head count every night. Was she playing to sold-out houses? You bet.

One night, Connie's father learned that Darin had suggested that the two lovers elope after one of her shows. Believe it or not, when Harry learned of this, he ran Darin out of the club while . . . waving a gun and shouting that Bobby would never see *his* daughter again. Close call for Darin all right. Bobby saw Connie only twice more; one time to deal with the TV series, *This Is Your Life,* and the other was a visit to the Apollo Theater to see James Brown and Ray Charles perform.

Meanwhile, career-wise, the two tracks produced by Atlantic Records founders, Ahmet and brother Nesuhi, for *Mack The Knife* won the Grammy Award in 1960, and Darin won "Best New Artist of the Year."

They followed *Mack The Knife* with a second entitled *Beyond The Sea,* which won another Grammy. Since that time, he was also honored with "The Grammy Hall of Fame" award. As both tracks were produced by Ahmet and Nesuhi, Bobby Darin was a hot commodity. He set all time attendance records in such places as the famed *Copacabana.* It was not unusual for Darin fans to line up around the block to get into his show.

Sammy Davis, Jr., a multi-talented and dynamic performer was quoted as saying, "Bobby Darin was the only person I *never* wanted to follow," after seeing his performance in Las Vegas.

Bobby Darin also played a significant role in fostering new talent, such as Richard Pryor, Flip Wilson and Wayne Newton. All three opened for him in his nightclub performances when they were virtually unknowns.

In 1973, Darin's poor health took a turn for the worse after he failed to take medication for his heart prior to a dental visit. He developed blood poisoning, which weakened his body and affected one of his heart valves. He entered Cedars-Sinai Medical Center for surgery to repair his heart valves. The surgical procedure was a success; however he died of complications in the recovery room.

One thing you can be sure of: Bobby Darin wanted to be a star. Not a small star, but a *big* star, and there could be no doubt about it – he deserved it. He had as many musical gifts as you could possibly dream of. Unfortunately, sometimes when reaching for that star, no matter the cost, can become your own undoing.

I felt sorry for Bobby Darin. My mind goes back to when something happened that was kind of sickening. Bobby and his manager had flown into Boston. It was an early morning flight, so that he could get on as many radio stations as possible for a promotional tour. The Boston Record distributor representative met them at the airport to do the rounds. Needless to say, the radio stations, as was their nature, heated the radio waves by announcing that Bobby Darin would be visiting their stations sometime in the afternoon.

Guess what. By the time they drove in from the airport there were fans at every station, and guess what else . . . there was another passenger besides Bobby Darin in the limo: a young and extremely good looking guy. I didn't know who he was. I needn't have worried; the kids knew.

At each stop, the kids weren't yelling, "Bobby! Bobby!" They were yelling out the name of this new boy just starting out in the business, "Fabian, Fabian."

Not much of a voice, but what a smile! At their first stop, it was obvious to Bobby that the fans were whipping themselves into a frenzy over Fabian (shown, left), Bobby was nonplussed. Not only did he not take it well, his language was abominable, and his actions proved just as bad.

He compounded the felony by pushing himself off the car seat and onto the floor of the limousine. I guess he thought no one would notice. Unfortunately, of course, he was wrong.

When they arrived at WBZ, there were such a throng of fans that they surrounded and started to pound on the car. Remember please, Bobby Darin was still in the fetal position on the floor. He told the driver to leave without coming into the Station. No thank you wave, no resolute cheer. Nothing.

Can you imagine in your wildest dreams, that one of the biggest names in the music industry, who reached Number 1 on the Pop Charts, was curled up on the floor of the limousine, and wouldn't get up and sit on the seat? Meanwhile, who is sitting on the seat and taking it all in? Fabian, of course, and **loving every minute of it.**

Connie Francis

I can't believe she's NOT in the Rock and Roll Hall of Fame.

She was born December 12, 1938. Her name was Concetta Rosa Maria Franconero, but most of us know her as Connie Francis.

Connie was a great kid and always took the time to send me very thoughtful thank you notes after each time she visited me for an interview on the radio. The note shown on the next page reads:

Dear Dave, Just wanted to let you know that I'll be in Boston Sunday evening, Feb. 20, Mon, 21, a part of Tues, 22ⁿᵈ, doing promotion for my new release (like back in the olden days).

I'll be taping a two-hour special for Look on TV [to be shown on the 31ˢᵗ] and spending some time with Paul Winnick and Dave Martus.

I'd love to be able to spend some time with you when I'm in Boston and reminisce about the days when the record business was just a little different.

Looking forward to seeing you, Dave.

Warm regards,

Connie

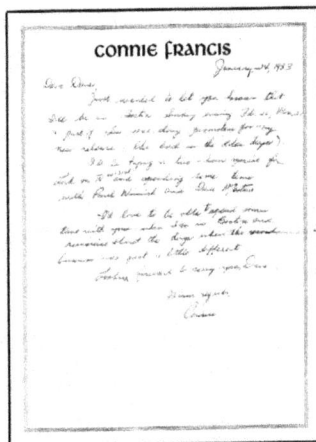

The last time I saw her was on a Sunday afternoon and I had just finished my taping of Community Auditions. She was in a suite that overlooked the Charles River in Boston with her mother and father. I had been invited to attend an afternoon brunch to catch up on old times. I hadn't seen Connie for a couple of years.

As I walked down the corridor to her party place, I wondered what she looked like now. After all, I reasoned, with the tough life she'd led, she might look pretty rough.

The door opened and there she stood, looking great. You could even say she looked delicious. It was a wonderful afternoon. Most of her other guests, around 20, had to leave and that, of course, made the afternoon even nicer. Quite frankly, I marveled at her appearance. For someone who had gone through unbelievable trauma, being attacked and raped in her hotel room in New York. In addition, in 1978, Connie underwent nasal surgery and completely lost her voice. She then went through several more surgeries and finally when she got her voice back, was forced to take vocal lessons in order to retrain her singing voice. She then returned to the touring circuit and the recording studio to begin work on an album titled *Who's Sorry Now*.

All this was short-lived. She was diagnosed with a mental illness which required extensive hospital care.

Just to give a sense of how prolific she has been, let's see how many of these songs you know: *Stupid Cupid, Who's Sorry Now, Among My Souvenirs, Lipstick On Your Collar,* and in 1960, she became the first female recording artist to have back-to-back number one hits with *My Heart Has a Mind of It's Own,* and *Everybody's Somebody's Fool, becoming the* first *female recording artist to achieve that standing.*

Starting at four years old, she performed in many venues, and eventually ended up on the Arthur Godfrey Amateur Hour, where, when he saw her practice performance, he told her to change her name to Connie Francis and lose the accordion. which she did immediately. Her performing career has spanned 68 years to date, and she is 72.

Among her notable honors are:

Performed in a Royal Command Performance before Queen Elizabeth II – 1963.

Top female Rock Artist on the Billboard Charts in the UK.

Recorded records in 15 different languages, topped the charts in the UK, and became a success around the globe.

Even at the height of the cold war, Connie's music was embraced by countries behind the Iron Curtain, although Rock and Roll was frowned upon by the Soviet Union. Yet, with all these accolades and successes, how can it be that my friend, Connie Francis, has **not** been inducted into the Rock and Roll Hall of Fame? And Connie, if you are reading this book, . . . a kiss from Davey and Suzan.

Peter Noone

I didn't like him. He was a rude, snotty punk.

What is to follow is a brief story that could be headlined several ways, but the one I've chosen is: *The short, irritating life of Pete Noone.* Good ole Pete, behind that buck-toothed smile was a rock and roll star of Machiavellian intensity. By the way, am I getting the point across that an average person could work up a real good hate towards him in short order?

First of all, his name was Peter Noone, but millions of rock fans all over the world knew him by another name because of a smash hit. People thought his name was

Herman, like in *Herman's Hermits*, like in *Mrs. Brown You've Got a Lovely Daughter*. I have to admit that it was a cute record, almost as cute as he thought he was.

As previously mentioned, I didn't like him, and I didn't like him the minute I laid eyes on him. One of the main reasons being, he was late for the first of two concerts we were holding at Canobie Lake Park in New Hampshire. Well anyhow, we were introduced backstage by his manager who explained that their flight was delayed, and I thought, *well, okay.*

Then I said, "Don't you think you ought to get ready? You have two shows to do, one at 8:30 p.m. and another one at 10 p.m."

Peter, being the only one sitting, jumped to his feet and said, "After we do the first show we've got to move up the last one to 9:30."

Ruth, my booking agent, responded, "According to the contract, there are to be two, one hour shows."

He turned to Ruth and said, "Shut up."

"Shut up or what?"

He said, "How would you like to be thrown into that lake?"

To which I said, "Get ready, 'cause you'll be the next one thrown in."

Then Ruth said, "I know why you don't want to honor your contract. You want to do only the one show, so you can get out of here and catch the last shuttle back to New York. But we're holding you to your contact for the full two performances."

Then, I got soft-hearted because I decided I wanted to get one complete show out of them and offered the compromise that they do their show from 9-10:30 p.m. as that would give them a shot at catching the shuttle in time. It took us about 10 minutes to settle the dispute, but I made a mental note never to be nice to any other British rock groups in the future. Well, maybe *The Beatles*, or at the outside, *The Rolling Stones*.

Angie Dickinson

Gee, what if she took off all of her clothes? . . . What would I do?

Did you know that the one and only Angie Dickinson would only allow the movie studio to lighten her naturally brunette hair to a honey blonde, and no lighter? I don't care. As far as I'm concerned, she could appear somewhere completely bald, and it wouldn't bother me a bit. It all started in 1953 when she placed second in a talent show. Soon after, she decided to pursue a career in acting.

In 1954, she made her television debut in an episode of *Death Valley Days*, and continued to capture roles in many of the television productions of the era.

In 1959, she appeared in *Rio Bravo* opposite John Wayne, her childhood idol, as a flirtatious gambler called "Feathers," who became attracted to the town's sheriff (Wayne). She became one of the more prominent leading ladies for the next decade, starring in such movies as *The Bramble Bush* with Richard Burton, and the original *Ocean's Eleven* with Frank Sinatra and Dean Martin.

During the 1960s and 70s, she expanded her motion picture career performing in such movies as; *The Sins of Rachel Cade*, as a missionary nurse tempted by lust; and opposite Maurice Chevalier in *Jessica*; as well as sharing the screen with friend Gregory Peck in *Captain Newman, M.D.*

She also played a femme fatale opposite future U.S. President Ronald Reagan in his last movie role, *The Killers*, based on a story by Ernest Hemmingway. She starred in movies opposite James Garner (of Maverick fame), Dick Van Dyke, and with Marlon Brando, Jane Fonda, Robert Redford, and Robert Duvall in *The Chase*. She performed with Rock Hudson in *Pretty Maids All in a Row*, and in 1974 as the tawdry widow, Wilma McClatchy, opposite William Shatner in *Big Bad Mama*.

The talk was all about town. I knew she appeared nude in several scenes of that movie, and was now attracting even more male fans. It was the promotion of that movie that led her to become a guest on my radio show at WBZ.

As I sat in the studio waiting, I kind of fantasized: *Gee . . . What if she decided to take her clothes off in the studio? What would I do? I don't know, but I think fainting would be in order.*

All of a sudden, the door swung open and there stood the lady of the hour, or two if she wanted. As we started the interview, I just couldn't help myself, and blurted out, "Your legs are legendary. In fact I can't figure out why volumes haven't been written about them."

She gave me a sweet smile and said, "Dave, you're just not reading the right books."

The hour-long interview flew by, and all I can remember is that I was captivated. I remember the last thing I asked her at the end of the interview, "Before you go, may I ask you to show me your legs?"

She smiled, and as she opened the door to leave, she turned to me and teasingly raised the hem of her skirt, all the way up to her thigh, then, blew me a kiss goodbye.

Wow. What a thrill! I'm a leg man.

Tony Bennett

"He is sensational and just about too good to be true!"

Anthony Dominick Benedetto was born August 3, 1926, and at the time this book was written, is still performing, singing popular music, standards, show tunes and jazz at 87 years young. In other words, he could sing it all. I suppose if he took the time, he could probably master the sound of a Mozart concerto, and sing that too. But, as you probably noticed, there is not much of a call for that these days. I'll tell you one thing that's for sure. If he were to sing such a concerti, I'm going to be there.

All this hero worship started back in roughly 1951, with his hit song, *Because of You,* and he recorded his signature song, *I Left My Heart In San Francisco,* in 1962.

Let's not forget his stellar performances as a youth in 1946 as a copy boy/runner for the Associated Press, nor as a singing waiter in various performing arts locations in Queens, New York.

After weathering the military for 90 days, Anthony was assigned as a replacement infantry man, the nicest job in the United States Army. Day after day, Americans would shudder to read of the heavy losses in the Battle of the Bulge. He joined the front line in March of 1945 and later would describe it as, "A front row in Hell." As the German Army was pushed back to their homeland, Tony

and his company saw bitter fighting in frigid conditions. During his time in combat, he narrowly escaped death several times and the experience made him both a patriot and a pacifist.

The military, at that time, was segregated, but on a trip to the mess hall he spotted an old friend from high school, and sat down next to his black friend. For doing so, he was demoted in rank and reassigned to grave duty. However, Anthony then got the opportunity to sing with the 314th Army Special Services Band, and in doing so, he met many other musicians who would have post-war careers as well.

The war over, Anthony returned home to New York City and was spotted by then popular singer, Pearl Bailey. She recognized his talent and asked him to be the opening act in her Greenwich Village show. She had also asked immensely popular comedian Bob Hope to attend her performance. After hearing Benedetto sing, Bob went backstage and asked Anthony to tour with him, but suggested he shorten his name, to Tony Bennett.

In 1952, Tony married artist and jazz fan, Patricia Beech. Together they had two boys, Danny and Dae who were to become very important to his career later in life.

In 1955, Tony released his first album, *Cloud 7,* and then followed up with a series of albums with more of a jazz flavor over the next eight years. At the same time, he built a strong following in the night club scene, performing in venues like Blinstrub's.

A table at Blinstrub's in Boston. Among those at the table are Charlie Applewhite (front left) and on the right (back to front) Joan Maynard, Dave Maynard, Tony Bennett.

He performed over a half dozen times at Blinstrub's, and if you look at my personal photo albums, you will see at least five pictures of Tony Bennett as he played Blinstrub's every year.

Stanley Blinstrub, owner of the nightclub, was a God-fearing Albanian. I remember one night at the club, it was a Saturday night, and Tony was on stage and I heard him say, "I know it is after midnight, but I'm going to sing this song for you anyhow." And you heard nothing for a second, and then all the lights went out. There was no microphone because someone shut all the electricity off.

Stanley had shut it off because he did not want to violate the Massachusetts Blue Laws that prohibited the club from staying open after Saturday midnight. Tony realized that someone had turned the microphone off, so he did the song anyway for the 1,400 people in the place, and then bought a round of beer for the entire house. Those 1,400 people soaked up a lot of sound, and Tony sang it without a microphone, projecting his voice and filling the room. – A lost skill, but one he still uses when he performs today. He sang a song called, *Lost in the Stars.* I'll never forget it, and he did it "au natural" in the pitch black.

The British invasion in 1964 signaled a decline in Tony's popularity, culminating in a desperate call to his sons, Danny and Dae, asking for help. Danny responded, immediately, signing on as his Dad's manager and began a rigorous promotion schedule, booking him in colleges and with more hip audiences like *The Late Night Show* with David Letterman, *The Simpsons*, and various MTV programs, while Dae helped with the production of his music. The boys efforts really paid off by the mid 1980s, and Tony's career experienced a resurgence. Tony's style of music was new to this latest generation of music enthusiasts. Young people who had never heard the tunes of Gershwin or Cole Porter. Tony Bennett was once again on top . . . top of the charts, and now the whole world was about to find itself in the palm of his hand.

His visited me many times on my radio show at WBZ, and even though there was a 20 year gap, from the 1960s to the 1980s, I told him, "We've got to stop meeting like this. People are beginning to talk."

I'll bet you didn't know this: He is an accomplished artist as well. He told me he had, from childhood, enjoyed drawing and even had sold some of his paintings under the name "Benedetto." When touring, he often sketches the view outside his hotel room. He has always found this a relaxing and satisfying respite from his rigorous schedule. He has published two books featuring his paintings, the most recent in 2007 entitled, *Tony Bennett in the Studio: A Life of Art & Music*, which became a best-seller among art books.

What can I say? How can so much talent reside in one individual?

He published *The Good Life: The Autobiography of Tony Bennett* in 1998, and was a recipient of The Kennedy Center Honors in 2005. Tony has sold over 50 million records worldwide and has received numerous Grammy Awards, the most recent in 2006 for "Best Traditional Pop Vocal." He continues to perform in around 200 shows a year, and when asked, has made it crystal clear he will *never* retire.

He also donates his time to numerous charitable causes. In fact he has been nicknamed "Tony Benefit" due to his dedication to those in need. In 2001, Tony and Susan Crow, founded a high school in Queens, dedicated to teaching the performing arts which, by the way, has an extremely high graduation rate. The school was named the *Frank Sinatra School of the Arts*, as a tribute to Frank Sinatra. Sinatra was quoted in Life Magazine in 1965 as saying, *"For my money, Tony Bennett is the best singer in the business. He excites me when I watch him. He moves me. He's the singer who gets across what the composer has in mind, and probably a little more."*

In September, 2011, Tony appeared on *The Howard Stern Show* to celebrate his upcoming 85th birthday, and to promote his most recent album, *Duets II*. The album paired him with Amy Winehouse, the last recording she made before her death. The album debuted at number one on the Billboard 200, making him the oldest living artist to reach the top spot, and incidentally, it was the first time he had a number one hit.

In December 2011, he appeared at *The Royal Variety Performance,* featuring the best entertainers in the world, in Salford, Manchester, England before Her Royal Highness, Princess Anne. At the time this book is being written, he is a spry 87, sensational, and just about too good to be true.

As I said, he is always busy performing, sketching, interviewing. He maintains one heck of a hectic schedule. He was always performing, except for this one occasion which I can share with you.

It was in the late 1980s and as I'm sure I've conveyed to you, Tony Bennett was Mr. Nice Guy. Tony was also, at the time, ultrasensitive about the size of his nose. He went on a radio station in Providence, Rhode Island. He got on the show with Ernie Anderson and, before they went on the air, Ernie said to him, "I understand you don't want us to make any mention, just to have some fun, about your nose."

Tony said, "Yes, I would really appreciate it if you didn't bring it up, especially as I get older. It's a pretty big beak."

Tony went on the air and Ernie started out the interview by saying, "Tony, I know you don't want me to bring it up, but I don't think you're right. You don't have such a big beak."

That was on the air. Tony proceeded to get up and walk out. Big mistake: That ended the interview.

Stephane Grappelli

As he played, it was as if he was in a trance. I was in awe. He was mesmerizing.

It was Virgil Thomson, an eminent music critic with The New York Herald Tribune, who in discussing the greatest classical instrumentalist of our time, was responsible for writing the glowing tribute of a genius. It was he who, when discussing the premier talents of Madame Wanda Landowska after a recent appearance at Carnegie Hall declared, "There was no doubt about it. Madame Landowska simply played the harpsichord and proved once again to these ears, that she played that fairly difficult instrument better than anyone played anything."

My sentiments exactly, with the exception of Stephane Grappelli, the premier jazz violin virtuoso.

Hey! Where do I get off comparing the brilliance of these two great artists? Landowska and Grappelli? Grappelli who? Stephane Grappelli, who back in the 1920s along with a gypsy guitarist by the name of Django Reinhardt, founded *The Hot Club* in Paris, France. Django performed alongside Stephane and accompanied him as a classical jazz guitarist.

You may remember that right in the middle of Django's career, a tragic fire spelled doom for his future. Django experienced burns so severe, it necessitated amputation of two of the fingers on his left hand, the fret hand, the hand that picks out the melody and frets the cords. Much to everyone's astonishment he relearned, in a very short time, to play the guitar in reverse.

They soon formed a quintet with Django's brother, Joseph, and Roger Chaput on guitars; and Louis Vola on double bass and created a new sound.

"It was a revolution to play jazz only with string instruments," Grappelli said. It was this new jazz style that took Europe by storm and eventually seduced the world for over fifty years.

After the war, Grappelli continued to attract audiences everywhere he went, and I was lucky enough to see him perform four times here in the United States. He almost never played with more than three or four other musicians. Hell, for my money he could strum a washboard and I'd love it. He would play his first set for about 20 minutes, and then went back to his dressing room for a break. I'm told that during that time he would partake of a little "weed."

The last time I saw him perform was at Scullers Jazz Club in the Doubletree Hotel, Boston, in 1990, and at the time, Stephane was 82 years old. Scullers is a small but intimate bistro overlooking the Charles River and frequented by many locals including students from Boston College, Emerson, Boston University, Harvard and MIT. It was definitely Stephane's house that night, and now the plot thickens. Stephane spoke very little English, but as he returned for his second set, which, by the way, was standing room only, and walked up to the microphone, he asked, "Vould you like to hear me play for you, a little piano?"

The crowd roared with approval. He sat down at the grand piano and began to play. One of the two fellows with the quintet edged over toward me and said, "Better keep your eye on him. He gets carried away sometimes."

As I stood there, I felt a big lump forming in my throat. Here's a man in his eighties, who's already done one set, and was about to perform another on his second love, the piano. As I watched him, I was in awe of his talent. I had heard he played the piano, and now he seemed oblivious to all around him. After he played for about 10 minutes, it was as if he were in a trance. His entire body was moving as he played up and down the keyboard. The look on his face was one of shear ecstasy. He wasn't just playing the music, he had become one with the music. His fingers were flying across the keys with Wagner, Beethoven, Bach and Mozart, one right after the other, mesmerizing and drenching the audience in his bliss.

After the performance was over, I spoke with one of his fellow musicians and asked, "How did you get him to stop?"

He then told me that Stephane had signaled him to approach, and asked, "Tell me something. Vat am I playing?"

"Remember, I told you, he sometimes gets completely carried away."

That was an understatement.

Stephane Grappelli was born in Paris, France, on January 1, 1908 and died from complications after hernia surgery on December 1, 1997.

I strongly recommend that you seek out his music and give yourself a real treat.

Trini Lopez

"If you don't play the selection I want, then I might have to send some friends up there to give you a good talking to," I told him.

I shall never forget opening the door to my office. It was a cold November afternoon and there stood the hottest new recording artist in America.

He looked at me and said, "How do you do. I'm waiting for Mr. David Maynard. My name is Trini Lopez."

I answered, "You are a lucky person. You've got him."

He walked over to me and stuck out his hand and, as he was shaking it, he said, "I'm also trying to locate Miss Ruth Clenott."

Then I heard Ruth say, "Oh oh. I'm in trouble," at which point Trini walked over to her and shook her hand as well.

He began to talk so fast that the only thing I could make out was, "I just wanted to thank you for playing my record." Well, that's just about all he said, over and over. "I just wanted to thank you for playing my record. I flew all the way here from Los Angeles just to thank you for playing my record."

The reason he came all the way to Boston was a reaction, at the time, to something I decided to do that caused quite a ruckus. I decided to do something that was not exactly what the recording company wanted. I always had Ruth listen to the albums that were given to us by the record distributors, and had her recommend what she thought would be the hit record for broadcast on the radio station. Ruth had an incredible ear for trends and what songs would catch the attention of the listeners. In fact, she had a record of choosing the hit songs from the last 30 albums we had received, and I wasn't about to doubt her recommendation now.

In this case, the "hit" record was not the one suggested by ABC Paramount. When I told Gordon Dinerstein, our record distributor, that I planned to play another selection on the air, he grimaced. What to do? So he called Sam Clark, then President of ABC Paramount Records in New York.

Could that be the same Sam Clark who, not so long ago, called his wife with Gordon Dinerstein in his office, and told his wife to get the bag of money out from under their mattress so he could sign Lloyd Price to a contract? Yes, one and the same.

Boy, did I get an earful from Sam. I told Sam I was going to play a different song, and that song was going to be the "hit" of the album.

He told me, "In a pig's ass it is!" It was 1966. Sam had been going through a dry spell, and had not had a hit for about six months. He told me in a threatening tone, "If you don't play the selection I want, then I might have to send some friends up there to give you a good talking to."

I told him, "I have a few friends too," and if he sent anyone up or if he came himself, I would make sure he got his block knocked off," and I then handed the phone back to Gordon.

Sam then asked Gordon, "Are you sure about this, Gordon?"

Gordon replied, "I'll take a chance because Ruth is *never* wrong."

I started playing the song. WBZ was the only station in the country playing it for the first three days. The song I am referring to was titled *Lemon Tree,* and within seven days, it was being played on 5,000 radio stations nationwide.

So there we were in the office; Trini, Ruth and I. He walked over to Ruth and said, "I have a tremendous idea. As a real sign of gratitude, let me use the chartered plane that I used to come to

Boston, and fly you back to Los Angeles so we can hang out and go to dinner."

I, knowing full well that Ruth would never fly even if Buck Rogers was the pilot, said, "I'm sorry. It is very generous of you, but neither Ruth nor I will be able to make it."

Then Ruth turned to me and said, "I think you've hurt his feelings."

"Hold his hand," I told Ruth, but he kept hold of her hand and made *no effort* to let go or to leave. It's nice to be irresistible.

We enjoyed a great lunch together at Locke-Ober in Boston. By the way, I had Lobster Savannah and headed back to the studio.

Trini asked me if there was anything he could do for me in California and I said, "No, not really, but thank you for asking."

That was Trini - very gracious and always the complete gentleman.

Trini Lopez was born in May 1937 in Dallas, Texas and I want to share with you a little bit about the Lopez family. Trini was a poor boy growing up in a Dallas barrio, and had barely enough food to go around for a family that included six children. The family, though, turned a bad situation into an opportunity, and his father, mother, sister and brother started playing music together to help make ends meet. Trini learned to play music on a $12 guitar his father had bought for him, and he became part of the family band. His first songs were in Spanish at local venues in Dallas. He became good friends with Buddy Holly and, after Buddy perished in an airplane accident, he got a call from Buddy's band, *The Crickets*, to come to Hollywood and be their lead singer. He thought he'd gotten his big break and went to Hollywood to play with the group, but unfortunately, that fell through.

When things didn't pan out with *The Crickets*, he found himself out of money and, out of desperation, decided that he had to do a solo act to earn enough money to support himself, and also send help back to his family. That decision got him the recognition to launch his amazing and prolific music career.

Trini has received numerous awards and recognitions for his musical and humanitarian contributions, such as:

- induction into *The International Latin Music Hall of Fame* in New York City, April 2003;
- A *Ten Diamond* award at the Los Angeles Music Awards for selling 100 million albums, 2007;

- A *Living Legend* award from the California State Senate, 2007;
- A *Lifetime Entertainment Achievement* award from the U.S. House of Representatives, 2007; and
- the Trini Lopez star dedication on the Las Vegas *Walk of Stars*, May 15, 2008.

Oh, by the way, *Lemon Tree,* was a hit. Some of his other well-known songs may be familiar to you; *If I Had A Hammer, America,* and the timeless, *La Bamba.*

Trini is still performing today. He has released more than 63 albums and is working on his 64th as this book is being written. It just doesn't get better than that.

Greer Garson

I was spellbound. It was just one of those unforgettable moments.

Greer Garson was discovered in 1932 by Louis B. Mayer of MGM Studios, in London. What a break for her, this beautiful red-headed actress, and certainly a huge step forward for Metro-Goldwyn-Mayer Studios.

Although she didn't sign a contract with the studio until late 1937, she was signed to play a part in a new motion picture, *Goodbye Mr. Chips*, for which she received an Oscar nomination; however, that year, Vivian Leigh won best actress for her performance in *Gone With the Wind*. Next she received critical acclaim for her performance in the 1940 film, *Pride and Prejudice*. The next year, 1941, she became a box office star, first in a Technicolor drama named, *Blossoms in the Dust,* which brought her the second of her seven best actress nominations. She won the award for Best Actress for her role as a strong British wife and mother in the middle of WWII in *Mrs. Miniver*.

The Guinness Book of World Records credits her with the longest Oscar acceptance speech, 5 minutes, 30 seconds, after which the Academy Awards instituted a time limit for acceptance speeches.

REMASTERED EDITION
ARCHIVE COLLECTION

GABLE'S *back*
and
GARSON'S
got him!

VICTOR FLEMING'S PRODUCTION OF

M-G-M's
Adventure

Joan BLONDELL
Thomas MITCHELL

Garson was partnered with Clark Gable after his return from the service in 1945. The film was advertised with a catch phrase, "Gable's back and Garson's got him!"

Gable retorted that the catch phrase should be "Gable put the arson in Garson!"

And she countered with "Garson's put the Able in Gable!" The movie, was named *Adventure*.

1967 was a golden year for her. In that year, she married a millionaire Texas oilman and breeder, and the couple retired to their Fork Lightning Ranch in New Mexico.

They made some headlines in the sports section of the paper by purchasing a U.S. Hall of Fame thoroughbred from the estate of Harry Guggenheim in 1971, and became highly successful breeders. They also maintained a home in Dallas where Garson founded *The Greer Garson Theater Facility* at Southern Methodist University. She also donated millions of dollars to *The Greer Garson Theater* at The Santa Fe University of Art and Design.

You know, it's funny. I knew every major male and female singer, top notch stars – the biggest stars of all – and yet it was some of the stars that weren't that big that enthralled me, and I had this beautiful lady on my radio show. It got to be about 11:30 in the morning, and as a commercial was playing, she leaned over and whispered to me, "Can I take you out to lunch?"

I came very close to fainting, and responded "Yes." As lunchtime approached, I became increasingly aware I had all of $1.06 in my pocket to go to lunch with her. Good thing she way picking up the tab.

We went to the Copley Plaza, just she and I, as her manager had to go somewhere else. I had the most delightful lunch with such a charming person. She knocked me overboard. It was one of those unforgettable moments. She was on my show promoting her new movie, *Random Harvest,* co-starring Ronald Coleman (shown) which eventually won an academy award for best movie of the year. I've met a lot of actresses, gone to a lot of lunch and dinner situations, but I was just spellbound. I was enchanted with her. Class! That's what I like, class, and believe me, she had it all.

Jimmy Stewart

Shortly before his 80th birthday, he was asked how he wanted to be remembered. He answered, "As someone who believed in hard work, in love of Country, in love of family and love of community."

One of Jimmy Stewart's lesser known talents was his homespun poetry. He once wrote a poem about his dog entitled *Beau* which he read on Johnny Carson's *Tonight Show*. By the end of the reading, Carson's eyes were welling up with tears. In addition to his poetry, Jimmy would talk about his avid gardening and – talk about putting your money where your mouth is – he purchased the house next door to his own home at 918 N. Roxbury in Beverly Hills so he could expand his garden.

Jimmy was born May 20, 1908. Over the course of his career, he starred in many films considered classics, and was nominated for five Academy Awards including a Lifetime Achievement Award. Some of his most notable films included, *Mr. Smith Goes to Washington, The Philadelphia Story, Harvey, It's A Wonderful Life, Rear Window, The Man Who Knew Too Much,* and too many more to mention. He was also represented on *The List of Leading Actors of the 100 Greatest Movies of All Time.* As of 2007, ten of his films have been placed into The United States National Film Registry.

Wait a minute and hold the presses. What is to come is a portion of Jimmy Stewart's life that you probably don't know about. His mother was an accomplished pianist and, intrigued by the piano, Jimmy asked for lessons. However, his dad discouraged that interest. Later though, his father was given an accordion as a gift, and Jimmy quickly learned to play. He used it to relax in-between takes during his acting career, and music became an integral part of his family life.

Once, at a cocktail party, I tried to get him to play, and guess what . . . he really could play. On this particular occasion, I was kind of proud of myself when asked to introduce him to the crowd. I steered away from the stock intros and introduced him as "The Master of the stomach Steinways." What the hell. I got a laugh out of it anyway. What followed was a short community sing along.

All this tuneful history took place at the Ritz Carlton Hotel in Boston. No, we didn't do *Lady of Spain* or *Melancholy Baby* for that matter, but we had fun. My heart leapt up when the concierge crept over to our table and said, "Mr. Maynard, Mr. Stewart wants to know if you would care to take a late supper with him and his fiancé in their suite after the cocktail party is over."

"Care to? Hell, you mean kill for," said I.

Ah me, where else but in this wonderful world of ours can a Brigadier General invite a PFC to dine together at the swankiest hotel in Boston? I think when I was discharged from the Army, my MOS (Military Occupation Specialty) number was next to the lowest there was.

Something very few realize was that, in my formative years, I had been the personal soda jerk to Gloria Hatrick Mclean.

Now you ask "Who the hell was Gloria Hatrick Mclean?" A lovely lady with some kind of dazzling smile, and back then, she always ordered the same thing, a Vanilla Coke, but on rainy days, a Cherry Coke . . . and now she was betrothed to Jimmy Stewart. This took a load off my mind, because to be quite truthful, I had an idea which I shared with no one, that soon to be Mrs. Jimmy Stewart was crazy about me.

As she spoke to me at the cocktail party, she looked me dead in the eye, seeming to get lost in my gaze. That I was sure of. This happened at least twice during the cocktail party. At one point I had made some kind of comment, and she answered it with her hand touching my sleeve. Now you can't tell me that a Vanilla Coke can do that to a woman. It must have been my charm!

Needless to say, I wasn't surprised at all when I didn't receive a Christmas card from the Newlyweds.

Now let's get back to Jimmy. The first member of the Hollywood establishment and also the first person to wear a U.S. Army Air Force uniform was . . . you guessed it . . . Jimmy Stewart. By the time Pearl Harbor was bombed, Jimmy had amassed over 400 hours of flight time. He quickly rose in the ranks to Captain Jimmy Stewart who served in the 445th Bombardment Group. Then he became Major Jimmy Stewart, and don't forget Colonel Jimmy Stewart in the Eighth Air Force. Is that the same Jimmy Stewart who served so valiantly in the Strategic Air Command? Yes, and he is also the man who served in the Vietnam War. He was awarded the Distinguished Service Medal, the Distinguished Flying Cross (twice), the Air Medal (four times), the Army Commendation Medal, the Presidential Medal of Freedom and the French *Croix de Guerre*. He was also tendered the rank of Major General in the Army Air Force Reserve, a move which must be sanctioned by the President of the United States!

Jimmy Stewart died July 2, 1997, at his home in Beverly Hills, California.

"America lost a National Treasure today," said then President Bill Clinton. "Jimmy Stewart was a great actor, gentleman, and patriot."

Years of military service to our Country: 1941 to 1968.

Richard Simmons

I wouldn't have believed it unless I had seen it with my own eyes! He had a certain sincere, tender streak towards his audience, which I found rather endearing!

I did a series of commercials promoting my show on WBZ and I wanted to include this as one of the highlights of that endeavor.

I guess I was one of the few TV watchers who hadn't ever had anything to do with Richard Simmons. I know I didn't. Only once did I see some nut cavorting around the studio shrieking at people and taking them to task for anything that came into his mind, and that was Richard. Successful he was, his target audience went as far as the eye could see. They were ladies, all of whom weighted over 200 pounds. He was not exactly an Adonis, but he would get out there in his striped gymnastic clothing, clothing that consisted of a tank top and cutie-pooh shorts, and get every-one's blood flowing. As a matter of fact, now that I think of it, I've never seen him wear anything else. Whether he was going to some-one's birthday party or a funeral made no difference; tank top and cutie-pooh shorts!

The day before he came to our studios, I was told by someone who worked for us that he had met Richard Simmons on a couple of occasions. I remember well, him telling me, "Get ready. He's a terror."

The next day, we were shooting some TV commercials with him, and I was in the makeup room being attended to by a makeup man, hair stylist and wig expert. I had not been informed by my producer that the promo was to feature me "in drag" for a portion of the commercial. That means I had some pretty funny clothes on, consisting of hot pink skin-tight tights with a top to match and a size 44DDD padded bra to boot, you know, just like Dolly Parton. *Boy*, was I attractive! There were a couple of full-length mirrors in the studio, and I couldn't pass one of them without sneaking a peek. A peek? Hell, I gave it a good long stare.

A young lady was in the process of fitting my wig, which made me look somewhat like Tootsie. I was beginning to look pretty devastating, when, from out of nowhere, arms lifted over his head, there in the doorway roared the beast, Richard Simmons. He turned to the hairdresser and said "Just what in *Hell* are you doing?"

"I'm fitting his wig."

"**Out**," he exclaimed.

Meanwhile the whole time I'm just sitting in my chair, mouth agape. I was trying to figure out his next move. What's to figure? His next move was to sit on my lap.

"I'll have you lookin' like a real queenie in one hour" he said. "Everybody else OUT!"

With a pleading tone in my voice, I said, "Please don't leave me alone with him."

"Oh, wise bastard huh?" he said.

"Fight fire with fire, buster," I said. Not very funny, but I was grasping at straws.

To be truthful, after that exchange of heated words, everybody calmed down and we re-sumed the taping session. Actually, it was a lot of fun. A couple of times Mr. Simmons tried to take over the Director's chair, but he was squashed the minute he got started.

Something worth noting: Watching Richard Simmons lecturing a bunch of overweight ladies, I must admit he had a certain sincere, tender streak towards his audience, which I found rather endearing.

Meanwhile, back to the taping of our commercial:

I was being chased around the studio by a bunch of hooligans. One of the bad guys enters Richard's set and shouts, "We're looking for Dave Maynard. Have you seen him?"

"I wouldn't tell you if I had," responds Richard.

Just then, I burst on the scene and shouted, "Help, Help, Hide me."

The next thing I know, I'm in drag, exercising with Richard's ladies. That was a mistake because we all started laughing so hard. Somehow I ended up with a huge pile of flesh piled on top of both me and Richard. I'm happy to report, no bones were broken nor adenoids ruptured. I'm also pleased to say, according to people who judge commercials, that this was one *funny* commercial, and boy, did people laugh. . . . It was a piece of cake!

Between that day and this, I've seen, lunched, and spoken to Richard five or six times. Has he calmed down? No. Is he going to? No. Why should he? He's had a swell enough time as it is. As far as 1'm concerned, one of his letters to me said it all: "I love you, I'll always love you, and there is nothing you can ever do to make me stop loving you, but you're still outrageous!

Andy Williams

To introduce him as an All American Boy, quite possibly might be going overboard with some people. Not me. I might be exaggerating a bit, but I doubt it.

First of all, as far as I can figure out, I've been friends with him for at least 50 years. I've been a fan of his for 50 years, but he owes me, I'm not talking about money, although I suppose if I was offered something really yummy, a BMW convertible, or something snazzy like that, I'd probably accept it. Otherwise, you couldn't tempt me.

Is it about time I tell you who I'm talking about. Here's sledgehammer clue #1:

He sang for the first couple of years with a male quartet.

It strikes me that this is not a giveaway hint, so here is musical clue #2:

He decided to dissolve the quartet and go out on the road as a solo artist.

The year was 1958, as I recall, and he was not an overnight success. Finally, the break came in the form of another talented guy who was a pianist of note, songwriter, comic and a very talented Master of Ceremonies. I was lucky enough to be watching a television show with a brand new cast, and if you missed any of the shows, on five nights a week, it was your loss. If you remember, the MC of the show was Steve Allen, and if you remember Steve Allen, you'll remember his stable of stars. They weren't stars yet, but they were going to be.

Do you remember Steve Lawrence? How about Eydie Gorme, or Don Knotts? Then there was Louie Nye, Tom Poston and one more: the guy who owes me – Andy Williams.

I interviewed Andy three or four times, and the last time was a remote we did in a shoe store on Washington Street, downtown Boston. After the interview was over, we stepped outside on the sidewalk to visit a little. He eased a pen out of his inside pocket and showed me his newest gadget. It was the latest thing. A pen that also had a clock in it. I, of course, admired this new gadget, and then he asked me if I would like one. I jumped at the chance and he proceeded to write down my name and address in a little notebook he carried and promised he would send me one in the mail.

I waited patiently for my new toy for over 50 years now. I've decided that my patience should be rewarded, so I figure the cost of the pen, plus interest, should make up the difference and should equal or exceed the price of a new red BMW convertible.

What do you think?

I can hear you asking, what was the name of the quartet that Andy Williams belonged to? Kay Thompson and the Williams Brothers was the name of the act. I bet you didn't know this: Guess who sang the soprano parts. . . . Andy Williams, the man who owes me a BMW.

Don Knotts (above).
Steve and Eydie (r)

By the way, I almost forgot. I'm sure there's a list somewhere of famous people who have a great deal to thank the *All American Boy*

for. For what? you ask. Well, here's a few; Tony Bennett, Bobby Vinton, Wayne Newton, Phyllis Diller, Robert Goulet, Ann-Margaret, and hey, don't forget Dave Maynard. Who's that? He's the very same person who was approached by a small boy at a restaurant in Framingham, who asked him to sing a song with him and his brothers. Gee, how did they ever know I'd say *okay*? (I found out that Andy had called them and told them I was coming to see them perform). Oh, how I wish I hadn't cried. . . . I was sensational. Barbershopping along with Donnie and . . . the Osmond Brothers.

One more thing. It has been said that in his time, Andy Williams was a member of the classiest night club act of all time, and later that evening I caught his show.

Do you think that anybody could make a marquee big enough to put these words on it?

Here Tonight . . . Maybe Longer . . . Kay Thompson and the Williams Brothers . . . Featuring Dave Maynard.

Paul Anka

Kathunk . . . Kathunk . . . Do you know what that is? . . . That's Paul Anka writing a song to the beat of the Merritt Parkway!

Question:

What do all these song titles have in common? *Calendar Girl* by Neil Sedaka; *Dream Lover* by Bobby Darin; *Stupid Cupid* by Connie Francis; *Take Good Care of My Baby* by Bobby Vee; *One Fine Day* by The Chiffons; *Chapel of Love* by The Dixie Cups; *Spanish Har-lem* by Ben E. King; *The Locomotion* by Little Eva; *He's a Rebel* by, The Crystals; The Johnny Carson Show Theme Song; *My Way* by Frank Sinatra *She's A Lady* by Tom Jones; *Put Your Head On My Shoulder*, and *Lonely Boy* by Paul Anka.

You've probably guessed by now. Chances are pretty good that all these songs were written by the same person, and that person was a 13 year old boy whose first recorded and published song was in 1957. His name, of course, is Paul Anka. In the 48 years I've been a part of the record business, I never met anybody who had more talent combined with an uncanny ability to always see the right side of everyone he met, and that's not an easy thing to say about the record business. Even though you meet a lot of nice people, you meet a lot of sharks as well.

Most of the sharks hang out in The Brill Building, located at 1619 Broadway, New York, N.Y. The sound produced in this building had more of a Latin feel, and produced songs that were written for the girl groups and teen idols of the day. Artists could go into one studio and write the song on a piano, go to another studio and give the music to an arranger and get it scored, and finally go to another office and get it published. It was one-stop shopping for talented songwriters and composers.

Then there was an office where there were one, two, or three guys just waiting for people to walk in with a record on some kind of tell-tale label, that is obscure. After the usual banter, the record was whipped onto the turntable, and they listened. They didn't even bother to listen to the other side. "Just play the A side again," they would say. "It's a hit!" All kinds of questions were shouted out like, "Who wrote it?" and "Is it for sale?" and "Play it Again."

I think you'll get a kick out of this. I was walking down 52nd Street in New York City on a Thursday afternoon with my wife. We were right in front of Eddie Condon's Jazz Club. All of a sudden, a little guy walks out from the club, followed by a 12 or 13 year old kid. I realized then he was a guy named Juggy Gayles, a promotion man for a couple of the publishing houses, and I guessed, without any help, that the kid with him must have had something to do with the record business. I had known Juggy for years. He was the type of guy who got everybody laughing the first 30 seconds after he walked in a room.

He spotted me and said, "Hi sweetheart."

Naturally, my attention was diverted by the youngster who was now swinging on the iron polls supporting the awning over the entrance to the club. Surely you remember doing that in your youth. Swing around right to left, then switch arms and swing from left to right. That's it.

I kind of wrote the kid off, turned to Juggy and said, "That your son?"

Juggy said, "Hell no, but let me tell you who he is. We've been up in New Haven all day, going to radio stations. I'm plugging this gem, this treasure. You know when you come down the Merritt Parkway there is a certain rhythm you can hear as you drive over macadam slabs. *Kathunk . . . Kathunk . . . Kathunk.* Dave, he wrote three songs to the beat of the Kathunks on the way down here." He told me, "If Pauley had had a little more time, he would have written three more."

Then he said, "We're gonna drive to Boston tomorrow, that's an eight-hour round trip, at three songs an hour; that's 24 more songs" Then Juggy called Pauley over and said, "Pauley, this is Mr. Maynard of WBZ radio in Boston. Sing him one of your songs."

Paul asked, "Which one?"

Juggy said, "Any one, you choose."

Well, when he finished, I was so excited, I said, "For God's sake, The Brill Building is just around the corner. Let's go!"

Paul Anka was born in Canada in 1941, and has written well over 900 songs and continues to perform to this day. *WOW!*

A short story now about the record business. I knew a housewife in Larchmont, N.Y., which is about 45 minutes from New York City. I chummed around with her son when I was a tenth grader. She invited me to lunch one day along with her husband and son in New York City. We ate at Luchows, which was right across the street from The Irving Berlin Music Publishing House. Her son and husband then proceeded to try to talk her into crossing the street to sell a song she had composed. At first she wouldn't go, but eventually she did. We were all sitting in the restaurant waiting, when she came out of the publishing house and ran back across the street, with what looked like a slip of paper. Even from a distance, I could see that the paper looked about the size of a check. Her hands were shaking as she pulled the paper from the envelope. Was it a rejection slip? No. A sale. And how much was the check for? A whopping $500. A nice jackpot for a nice lady. And, you ask, the name of the song? The classic *How Deep Is the Ocean,* or as my friend's mother, Janet Champion, originally titled it, *How Much Do I Love You.*

Danny Kaye

He was the most talented man I ever met!

You know, it's rather difficult when writing a piece about David Daniel Kaminsky because there is so much to tell. He was an actor, singer, dancer, comedian, and an all-around hell of a guy.

I've had the privilege of watching him perform a number of times, and he is one of the few who could walk out on a stage anywhere and entertain for hours on end.

The last time I saw Danny Kaye, he gave a two hour performance, splitting the time right down the middle with another very talented and funny man whose name you may recognize . . . ahhh, the wonderful Senor Wences. Senor Wences was the little man who made people laugh by painting his thumb and forefinger with lipstick to facilitate the making of a mouth, and with the proper movement, became a talking face entertaining millions on television shows, such as, *The Ed Sullivan Show*.

Danny Kaye came from Brooklyn and was knocking about the Big Apple, keeping himself alive as an insurance investigator, and later as a clerk in a dental office. As an insurance investigator, he made an error that cost the company $40,000 and was fired. Then he was fired by the dentist, when it was discovered that while the staff was at lunch, he was using the dentist's drill to redesign the woodwork around the office.

Danny's first break came in 1933 when he joined a three man vaudeville dance act called *The Three Terpsichoreans*. The act toured the United States and then got a contract to perform in the Orient. The act then stopped in Osaka, Japan, where they were to perform on their way back to the U.S. Unfortunately, a hurricane hit the city that day and by performance time they were in the grip of a ferocious storm. With the theater full of patrons, the power suddenly went out, and as you might imagine, the audience was experiencing high anxiety. In an effort to keep everyone calm, Kaye went on stage, his face lit by a flashlight, and sang every song he could think of, as loudly as he was able.

That experience of trying to entertain a non-English speaking audience was what brought him to create the gestures, songs, and facial expressions which eventually made him so famous.

Once, while traveling with his daughter, Dena, in Japan, he used his gesturing skills in an effort to order dinner at a local restaurant. Unfortunately, his skills did not always meet with the greatest of success. As Dena described it, he tried to gesture what he wanted by flapping his arms, clucking and doing his best imitation of a chicken. The waiter nodded with understanding and quickly returned with two raw eggs.

Upon his return to the States, jobs were in short supply. However Danny managed to snag a position appearing with fan dancer, Sally Rand. His job was to be the keeper of the fans. Just in case she dropped one, he would come to her rescue with another. Hey, pretty good work if you can find it. But then again, money isn't everything. Health and happiness account for at least . . . 2%.

Kaye also found time to star in a radio program of his own, *The Danny Kaye Show*, in 1945.

I remember the show had a stellar cast, including big band leader, Harry James; Eve Arden, of *Our Miss Brooks* fame, and lord knows how many more who appeared in guest spots.

Kaye performed in over 20 movies. My personal favorite was *The Secret Life of Walter Mitty*. Tah . . . pak . . . it . . . tah, Tah . . . pak . . . it . . . tah, Tah . . . pak . . . it . . . tah. Who could tell what else would spring from his fertile mind.

Danny had one character he shared with friends and family, but never with the public, and that was *Kaplan*. Just who in the hell was Kaplan? Kaplan was the owner of a rubber company in Akron, Ohio. He didn't have a first name, and even his wife called him just Kaplan. He was an illiterate, pompous character who could take you "downtown" for a couple of hours! (That means he can overwhelm you with talk for a long time.)

Danny also appeared at the London Palladium Music Hall in 1948. He roused the Royal family to shrieks of laughter, and was the first of many performers to turn English variety into an American art form. Life Magazine described his reception in London as "worshipful hysteria," and noted that "the Royal family, for the first time in history, left the Royal box to see the show from the first row of the orchestra."

Music of all types; radio, television, special concerts, there was no stopping Danny Kaye. He, could do anything and everything. For example, he often claimed an inability to read music, yet was a talented conductor and said to be gifted with perfect pitch. This orchestral prowess was brought to the attention of Dimitri Mitropoulos, conductor of the New York Philharmonic Orchestra. Immediately following a guest appearance by Kaye, Mitropoulos remarked, "Here's a man who is not musically trained, cannot even read music, and gets more out of my orchestra than I ever have."

Like many in the film business at the time, Danny Kaye was an aviation enthusiast. He became seriously interested in learning how to fly in 1959, and decided to pursue his pilot's license. In short order he qualified for his multiengine license, then certified for a commercial pilot's license and flew every type of aircraft except military. He may not have flown military aircraft, but he spent plenty of time entertaining the troops during WWII.

In his spare time he also took up golf, but, although he was recognized as an excellent player, he found he simply did not have the time to devote to that hobby.

In 1952, Danny hosted The 24th *Academy Awards*, the same year I started in the broadcasting business. I remember because, at that time, the Oscar ceremony was broadcast only on the radio. Telecasts of the Oscars started much later, in 1969.

Kaye entered the world of television big time in 1956 through the CBS show, *See It Now*, with host Edward R. Murrow. Danny then combined his talents with a 50,000 mile, ten country tour as the UNICEF Ambassador raising over $5 million for hungry children through music, humor and a lot of laughs.

In the late 1970s, Kaye tore a ligament in his leg, but went on with the show, appearing with his leg in a cast and raising all kinds of hell on stage in his wheelchair. By then he was experienced as a wounded performer, having done the same kind of thing on his television show in the 60s when his right leg and foot were seriously burned at home in a cooking incident. Again, he was in a wheelchair, but predictably, brought the house down.

By the way, as long we are on the subject of Danny Kaye and cooking, in his later years he took to entertaining at home as a chef. He even had a special stove installed outside on his patio. The stove was specifically designed for preparation of Chinese cuisine, which he had learned to love from his early years in the Orient. The stove was equipped to cook with woks and had all the necessary accoutrements needed to prepare the desired dishes to perfection. Chef Kaye also taught – did you get that – taught . . . Chinese cooking classes at a San Francisco restaurant in the 70s. Again he was recognized as a master chef. The theater and demonstration kitchen beneath *The Culinary Institute of America* in Hyde Park was named for Kaye. He also received *Les Meilleurs Ouvriers de France* award. He was the only non-professional chef to ever achieve such an honor.

With all those accolades, one might think everything he did turned to gold. However, not all of his efforts in the kitchen turned out so well. I don't want to burst your bubble, but want to tell you about one bread-making incident.

After flying to San Francisco for a pet recipe for sourdough bread, he came home and spent hours preparing the loaves. When daughter Dena asked him how the bread turned out, Kaye tried to show her by hitting one of the loaves on the kitchen table. The bread was unharmed, but the table did not survive the demonstration. The bread was so hard, it actually chipped the table.

I'm having a bit of trouble recalling everything I learned about Danny Kaye after he spent a couple of magnificent hours with me on my show. I remember the day well though. He was to arrive at the studio around 2 o'clock, but, you know, I'll tell you a funny thing, that at about 1:30 p.m. . . . and I almost never get to use this word . . . a metamorphosis took place in the studio. I swear to God there was a complete change in the atmosphere in the studio. I reasoned correctly that Danny Kaye must have arrived.

Your friend Dave couldn't think for a minute what to say. I was drawing a blank. Want to take a guess what I decided to say? I took a deep breath and said, "Hi Danny." You could tell I was really quick on the uptake with that greeting.

What do you think Danny did? He burst into raucous peals of laughter. All of a sudden, I wasn't nervous anymore. We got behind the microphones and we were off, talking about everything. He knew everything. We talked about the many times he visited Japan, and the fact that he didn't speak Japanese didn't seem to bother him at all, so I didn't let it bother me either. He talked a lot about flying, and more than anything else, he had stories to spin, but very little about himself. Danny Kaye was a natural storyteller with the uncanny knack of saying the right thing at the right time. Have you ever seen anybody get a laugh with Shirley Temple as the straight man? Easy; just follow Danny Kaye around.

By this time, the control booth in front of us was jam-packed with just about everyone who worked at the station. Then I put my foot in it. I glanced up at the clock and said, "Gee, five minutes before 3 o'clock."

He looked at me and said, "So?"

I said, "So nothing. News time is at 3 o'clock. Can you stay until after the news?"

He replied, "No, the HELL with the news!"

Then I said, "You see that crowd of people in the control room? One of them is the General Manager, and you can tell which one, because his face is changing color very quickly . . . to red!"

The staff was shooting me all kinds of signals. I didn't know what half of them meant and a couple of them were dirty.

I looked up at the clock, and with two minutes to go, I didn't know what to do, so I punched the intercom and asked the newsman, who was sitting in the newsroom waiting patiently, "What do you think Hank? Would you be mad if I don't do the news?"

He replied, "I'll be mad at you if you do!"

I bolted back to the microphone, saluted the control room and said to our general manager, "Arthur. What's your final ruling?"

Arthur Haley nodded *yes*, but said, "Just try not to miss the 4 o'clock."

The Monkees

The critics of The Monkees observed that they were simply the Prefab Four, "a made-for-TV knockoff of The Beatles." "The Monkees are the Marx Brothers of rock and roll," said John Lennon. "I never miss an episode!"

Ah, yes. I remember it well. I sat there in my studio trying to resurrect a certain feeling that I had. Everything had been going along so smoothly. There are some days you feel sharper than others, so I just turned on the microphone and let er rip.

I had played three or four songs that were not yet hits, but I knew were going to be. I knew within the next half hour or so, I was going to be joined by the hottest rock group, well . . . maybe the second hottest.

All of a sudden, my dreaminess was jolted and the group I'd been waiting for burst through the door of the station. Suddenly total bedlam broke out. They were rowdy, and racing up and down the hallway. They came into my studio for the inter-view, and about halfway through, they went pretty much crazy. All four guys talking at the same time and nobody listening, including me, making them impossible to interview. I was very patient for a short while, but before I knew it, I started to yell back at them. In my newfound reality there were these

loudmouthed, ill-mannered brats, and, quite frankly, I thought I was justified in the way I handled the situation.

I distinctly remember calling one of them a "stupid schmuck."

What happened next is one for the books. I announced to the listeners that I was going to shut off the microphone for about a minute to see if I could get the interview under control. If anything, the situation just deteriorated, and at that point, I asked my producer to call the Brighton police, located just four buildings away.

The police arrived and came directly to me and asked what was the matter.

I said, "The Monkees."

"The Monkees? I like them and their music," said the officer. "Where are they?"

"You can hear them from anyplace in the building," I said. "I don't want them arrested or anything like that. I just want them out."

They walked out and my producer walked in. He said, "Have you gone crazy?"

"Yes, I have," I responded.

The road manger came in and apologized for the group and I had the suspicion he was going to have a talk with them later. Oh, by the way, I forgot to introduce each of them to you. They, ladies and gentlemen, as you know, were The Monkees, and their group consisted of Davy Jones, a nice British lead singer, Mickey Dolenz, Peter Tork and Michael Nesmith.

The idea of a television show featuring a rock and roll group was the brainchild of Bob Rafelson and Bert Schneider after they saw the film *A Hard* Day's *Night*. They thought they could market the records from the show so in 1965 they ran an advertisement in *Daily Variety* and *The Hollywood Reporter* to cast the band.

Don Kirschner, the head of music at Screen Gems, was asked to generate some music for the pilot that would be the signature songs of *The Monkees*. No one at the Brill Building in New York seemed interested in this endeavor, so Don asked Tommy Boyce and Bobby Hart to work on the project.

A lot of musical chairs happened in their development, not the least of which was that the members of the group were not playing their instruments with any level of proficiency and needed to practice constantly just to present the group well when their band's first record was released in August of 1966, just a couple of weeks prior to the TV show's debut. In addition, because the four were real pranksters, when they got together to record their music, they spent too much time joking around which made it difficult to get down to the task at hand.

Somehow, however, everything worked out because just before the TV show premiered, NBC and Columbia Records, had the first Monkees hit on their hands.

Eventually, the group encountered "artistic conflicts" with Don Kirschner and parted ways. They went on tour and managed to charm the audiences in their first live performance in Phoenix, Arizona, in 1967. They later did a tour of the U.S. and the U.K., as well as Australia and Japan, where they were met with the kind of adulation the Beatles enjoyed worldwide.

The Beatles' John Lennon was quoted as saying "The Monkees' humor was the Marx Brothers of music," and hosted a party for them when they toured England. Lennon also said, "I never missed an episode."

They later collaborated with Tork, who played Paul McCartney's banjo on George Harrison's *Wonderwall Music* cuts.

The Monkees had a number of international hits and are still played on oldies radio stations with hits such as: *Hey, Hey We're The Monkees, I'm A Believer, I'm Not Your Steppin Stone, Daydream Believer, Pleasant Valley Sunday, Last Train to Clarksville,* and have sold over 65 million copies. Not bad for a bunch of boys I was ready to strangle.

Johnny Most

He wasn't just a basketball announcer, he was different. He was Johnny Most!

To be truthful, I can honestly say that January 3, 1993, the day that Johnny Most passed away was most unforgettable. Johnny was the play-by-play Celtics basketball announcer for 37 years, from 1953 to 1990, with his raspy, grizzly-bear voice and delivery. You frequently hear it expres-

sed that he was a standout sports legend, but he wasn't just a basketball announcer, he was differ-ent. He was Johnny Most.

He didn't put on any airs. What you heard is what everybody got. He was also known for his somewhat strange mode of dress. He dressed like a hobo trying to go straight. In fact, compared to Johnny Most, Columbo would be the Beau Brummell of sports. Absolutely nothing he wore matched.

Johnny Most was born in June of 1923. Oh, how well I remember the first couple of days following his death. You couldn't find a bar or bistro where there weren't small, but avid basketball fans spinning yarns and swapping memories and stories about the good stuff, the Johnny Most stuff.

Some memorable Most-isms that were recounted included, "High above courtside, I'm watching the Boston Celtics get ready to do basketball battle."

Of course, the most memorable call occurred during the final moments of Game 7 of the 1965 NBA Eastern Division Finals – the play that clinched the Boston Celtics victory:

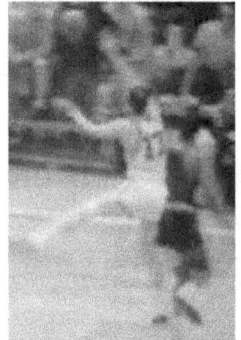

> "Greer is putting the ball in play. He gets it out deep and *Havilcek Steals it* ! Over to Sam Jones. ***Havilcek stole the Ball***! It's all over! Johnny Havilcek is being mobbed by the fans. It's all over! Johnny Havilcek stole the ball! Oh, boy, what a play by Havilcek at the end of this ballgame! Johnny Havilcek stole the ball on the pass-in. Oh, my, what a play by Havilcek!

Never was there a more biased play by play announcer, of course, always in the Celtics favor. We all loved him for that.

Just a few examples of things that happened:

About 20 years ago, I was in the New England Baptist Hospital. I had just had double knee replacement surgery and was on the mend. My nurse came into the room to administer some scheduled physical therapy, and boy was I ever not looking forward to it.

All of a sudden, she blurted out, "Did you know that Johnny Most is here in the hospital?"

"You're kidding," I said. Little did she know, I had already made plans to pay a little visit to Johnny just to show him how helpful I could be from my wheelchair.

As soon as my physical therapy was over, I hopped into my wheelchair and headed to his room. He was just regaining consciousness from the anesthesia, slowly opened his eyes, and there I was, right in his face.

The first thing he saw, of course, was me, and the first thing he said was, "Aw Shit."

"I wanted to be the first one to see you post op," I said. I think I was a big shock to him. After all, he probably expected to see his wife when he first opened his eyes, but I beat her to it.

Here's another incident; *Bing, Bang, BOOM.* I remember we received a note from hospital staff that Mr. Most, contrary to the rules and regulations, was in the process of lighting a cigarette (or something similar) while on oxygen, when the flame and the oxygen got together on his face, and he nearly blew it off. I visited him in the hospital, after he began to heal, and the first thing he did was push a cigarette between his lips, unlit of course, and boy did we laugh.

Johnny never spent very much time talking about his past. You could have knocked me over with the proverbial feather when I found out that he was an aerial gunner during 'the big war,' and flew 28 combat missions over Europe, earning seven medals. Shortly after VE day, as his unit broke camp, Johnny wandered up a nearby hillside to visit a graveyard filled with American flags. Johnny the poet penned these somber words:

> "I stood among the graves today and swept the scene with sight.
> And the corps of men who lay beneath looked up to say goodnight.
> The thunder still, the battle done, the fray has passed them by,
> And as they rest forever more, they must be asking, *Why?*"

Lou Monte

It was a typical day at the radio station for me and then, in strode Lou Monte!

Occasionally, a novelty song would slip by, like Lou Monte's *Che La Luna Mezza Mare.* I'll never forget the day he raced into the studio shouting, "It's A Hit. . . . Dave, It's A Hit!"

I responded, "I already played it today, Lou."

"Screw that," he said. "You can play it more than once. It's a hit, and I've got something nice for you."

"I don't need something nice. I'm playing your

record anyhow," I said.

At that precise moment he decided to throw himself down into a chair next to me and fling his feet up on the desk, and mumbled to himself, "Yeah, . . . I've got a hit."

It was then I noticed he had a huge lump on his ankle. "Lou, what's the matter with your ankle?" I asked. "You might have a doctor take a look at that."

"And you know what he'll see? Come take a look," he said.

Have you ever seen what a lump a couple of thousand dollars makes when it's rolled up like a snowball in a sock? Lou then explained to me that he was from New York and, as a precaution to keep from being robbed, he would roll his money around his ankle under his sock.

We decided to go out to lunch to celebrate his new hit. Later, you should've seen the look on the waitress's face when he pulled out that wad of green stuff. "It's a hit. . . . It's a hit. . . . It's a hit.

Chapter 5

Politics

As the adage goes, what goes around, comes around, and this chapter definitely confirms all that and more. Somehow, no matter how confusing politics can be, there is always room for a little laughter. I hope these stories will encourage that, no matter what weird things seem to happen in the political arena.

James Michael Curley

I remember the day oh so well. It was the middle of October, 1953, in Boston, a warm and beautiful fall day. As I strode leisurely along, I became aware of a small crowd. I heard one or two raised voices, which were in some kind of a disagreement. My time was free. I had already put in an hour of ogling the ladies of fashion who always seemed to find their way onto the windiest corner in Boston (The intersection of Tremont and Boylston Streets), right in front of the old Hotel Touraine. Ah, yes. I was a leg man back then, and come to think of it, still am.

I could see one or two guys, maybe three, and according to a couple of people standing by, it seemed that they were arguing over who had the

right to the cab they had flagged down. Oh yes, I forgot to tell you one of the participants was a woman. The two guys were both well-dressed and fat. I hate well-dressed fat men. The lady was average height and, from what I could hear, seemed to be holding her own in the argument. The fact that she was, and I'm guessing now, about six months pregnant, certainly was reason enough that I should get involved. As it turned out, that woman was my wife. As I started toward them, I felt a hand on my arm and heard a very calm voice that said, "I'd advise you not to get involved."

I said, "But that's my wife there."

He said, "Yes, but it's almost all over. Here comes James Michael and he'll take care of everything. You're not from Boston are you."

I replied, "No."

He said, "James Michael is one of the most successful politicians in Boston, and probably the entire country."

By the time James Michael was finished dressing down the guys, he had extolled the virtues of motherhood, the merits of chivalry, the love of one's country, and the prospect of becoming an indisputable hero in the eyes of their own mothers for their demonstrated compassion towards a damsel in distress.

The crowd went wild, and there, in the middle of it all, was James Michael Curley, flower in his buttonhole and beaming.

There are probably quite a number of people who know nothing about the political life of James Michael and the political lives of such names as Huey Long or Warren G. Harding (Teapot Dome scandal). There are undoubtedly dozens more, but compared to our busy Irishman, they're next to nothing.

Let's take a look at him. He led an active life. James Michael Curley was born November 20, 1874, and died November 12, 1958. He was beloved by the working class and poor. They saw him as a man who would stick his neck out to help those in need. In 1904, James Michael Curley was convicted and sent to prison for fraud. The charges came when it was discovered that he and an associate took the civil service exams for two men in their district to help them get jobs with the post office. While serving his time in jail, James Michael ran for Boston's Board of Aldermen . . . and won!

Back in 1910 when he was in his twenties and a member of the Boston Board of Aldermen, he ran for U.S. Congress. He faced an uphill battle running in a three-man primary for the Democratic nomination. He defeated both challengers and went on to win the general election against his Republican opponent by a substantial margin.

James Michael, the charismatic politician, served four terms as Mayor of Boston, serving from 1914-18, 1922-26, 1930-34, and 1946-50.

During his second term in Congress, his popularity in Boston remained high, even though he was slapped with a felony indictment in 1941 for influence peddling, a charge that stemmed from his involvement with a consulting firm to secure, of all things, defense contracts . . . right in the middle of WWII. He then ran successfully for Mayor . . . from jail, with what proved to be a dazzler of a slogan; "Curley Gets Things Done."

I'll say. Undoubtedly his slogan was one of the major reasons that helped him get elected to a then unprecedented fourth term as Mayor.

Oh, I almost forgot. The race for Mayor was a three-way contest and James Michael Curley won the election with 45% of the vote. At the urging of the Massachusetts delegation, President Truman then commuted his sentence so that he could serve his term as Mayor. A huge crowd greeted Curley upon his return to Boston with a big brass band playing, *Hail To The Chief.* Upon his return to office and in a fit of excessive pride, he told reporters, "I've accomplished more in one day back in office than what has been accomplished in the five months during my absence." Of course, he failed to mention that his second-in-command, who he left in charge while in jail, had been instructed to put off any decisions until his return.

When he ran for Mayor the next time, he was defeated by his opponent – his trusted lieutenant and second in command.

In the long and colorful life of James Michael Curley, there are at least a thousand stories.

One that sticks in my memory would be, *The Coat*, and what a coat it was. It must have been made of a thousand pelts. Of course, I exaggerate . . . a bit. I'm sure it was his pride and joy. He wore it at work and at play. I'm speaking of a full-length raccoon coat, which he wore almost all the time, especially outdoors through those cold brutal winters, and always on the campaign trail

Curley in his raccoon coat greeting Richard Cardinal Cushing during the 1945 Mayoral campaign.

He was heard to say to one of his campaign workers as he was riding along in his chauffeur-driven limousine wearing his famed coat, "This is it. This is how to campaign. You know, they're not lucky enough to have a raccoon coat like me."

He would jump out and start chatting to his constituents the minute the limo stopped, and was known to give twenty to forty speeches a day. I remember well, a native of *Southie* told me about one of his vintage stops:

As he explained, James Michael was sitting in the tonneau (a specialized back-seat of his limo) and he was in the habit of throwing off his coat while caught up in the fervor of his stump speech. As he spoke, out of the corner of his eye, he noticed his precious coat moving away out of the tonneau of his limo. Now, picture this. James Michael Curley at the helm, in full campaign mode, roaring, raging and barnstorming the city, and something or someone was quietly trying to steal his prized coat. But, without missing a beat, killed two birds with one stone. While delivering his speech, he suddenly shouted out to the crowd, "Get the son of a bitch that's trying to steal my coat!" In the seconds that followed he coat was safely secured, and the would-be thief swiftly apprehended. Meanwhile, James Michael ended his speech with a standing ovation. . . . Just a typical day on the Curley campaign trail.

James Michael was a charismatic politician who led a charmed life.

In 1955, Curley ran for Mayor of Boston for the last time. It was his 10th time running for office. Although he did not prevail, his notoriety and legendary gift of gab continues to be fondly remembered. His death in 1958 led to one of the largest funerals in the city's history.

If you are ever driving on The Jamaicaway, across the street from the pond, look for the shamrock purple shutters on his former residence, now an historical landmark, and check out the two statues he is honored with; one at Faneuil Hall showing him standing and giving a speech, campaign button in his lapel, and one across from Boston City Hall showing him seated on a park bench.

As Paul Harvey would say, "And now you know the rest of the story."

Thomas P. "Tip" O'Neil - 1955

What Goes Around, Comes Around

WBZ TV asked me to cover the Democratic Election Headquarters at Lowenstein's Furniture Store on Boylston St. and I said, "What? Are you crazy? I am a disc jockey; I'm not a newsman."

They said they thought I could handle it anyhow.

"Well," I said, "I'd just feel like a fish out of water."

Then they said, "Well, you're gonna do it."

So I said, "Okay."

It was kind of an *or else*!

So, I dwelled on anything political for the next three weeks, because I didn't want to do anything like that, without some background. I tried to learn as much as I could, but I was scared and I looked it. As I was waiting for John Kennedy and Jackie to arrive, I did a couple of pretend interviews. Suddenly, I heard this voice from behind my ear that said, "There are only two people outside here that know how nervous you are. You're one and *I'm* two, and I don't give a damn, and neither should you."

He walked away, and I will never forget it. He had a very positive walk and he had that shock of brown hair.

I asked one of the crew standing next to me, "Who was that?"

He responded, "That was Thomas P. O'Neill, otherwise known as 'Tip,' and he's going to take over Jack Kennedy's seat in Congress, when Jack is elected to the Senate."

I will never forget what he said: "It's me and you, and I don't give a damn."

There were five or six times I asked him to help with situations, and learned that, "When you want something done, go to Tip."

August 20, 1988 -Tip O'Neill- Going away dinner

It was 1988 and I can tell you some things about Tip. I was invited to sit at the table at Tip O'Neil's going away dinner and I flew down to Washington, D.C., with a couple of guys. Everyone in attendance was given an honorary "Tip O'Neil magic putter," which gave me great luck, and luck to anyone who used it down here in Florida. However, before we sat down at our table, I said to the gentleman sitting to my right, "Nobody knows who you are here, so it would probably be in your best interest to be nice to me." My seatmate was Doug Flutie, then Quarterback for the NFL New England Patriots. You know I'm kidding!

Impromptu Pizza Tasting Contest - 1993

I decided to have an impromptu Pizza Tasting Contest. It was a contest that would only last for one month with pizza makers from

the Greater Boston area to call in for an assigned day that wanted to compete. Quite a number of people showed up to taste the free pizza. On one of the days, my guests were Tom Landry, the Coach of the Dallas Cowboys at the time who had stopped by to promote his latest book.

Do you want to know who the next celebrity was? I felt rather honored that it was Benjamin Netanyahu, Prime Minister of Israel.

These two were, of course, the judges for that day. (The Prime Minister hadn't planned it that way; that's not why he showed up). He was scheduled to go on the show anyway, but that pizza was coming in hot and heavy, and I was feeding everybody, so I did an interview with him while we ate pizza. They both had a good sense of humor. I will never forget the look on the Prime Minister's face when he said to me, "Do I get a piece of pizza too?"

I burst into tears. . . . Just kidding.

By the way, the *Best Pizza* award went to Foodees, run by four former CEOs who had lost their jobs in the last economic downturn, and opened a pizza shop in downtown Milford, New Hampshire, and, by the way, received that distinction every year from 1993 to 1996.

Payola: Dave takes on The U. S. Congress - Feb. 20, 1961

It felt like it was Christmas time. I was rather surprised and I'll tell you why. Somebody sent me a television set at the station, and I naturally said to my secretary, "Who sent me that? Who's it from?"

She said, "Perry Como."

This proved to be a prelude to the entire Payola affair, although I never played a song I wasn't sure would be a hit. Working as a disk jockey on Saturday nights made sure of that. I put each new song to a vote. Kids have an unfailing instinct to pick the hits . . . every time.

Another well known name in the record world used to commute by boat from Stamford, Connecticut to Manhattan each day, and complained that his 18-foot skiff was too small for the choppy waters, and so was his outboard motor. Guess what *he* got for Christmas . . . St. Patrick's Day . . . his birthday . . . Washington's Birthday . . . and Bastille Day. By the time he was finished, he had a whole fleet of yachts. . . . Just kidding.

It was 1961 and the U.S. Congress was investigating Payola in the record industry. *Payola* was a word that just about every American knew the definition of. What it meant was commercial gift-giving in exchange for a commitment to play specific recordings on the radio, often referred to as "Pay for Play."

Gordon Dinnerstein owned a distributorship for new record releases. His office was on Huntington Avenue in Boston. We went on a golf trip to The Pinehurst Golf and Country Club in North Carolina. We had just walked off the course and I said, "Boy, what a day."

At the 19th hole, we downed a whisky sour. Excuse me, did I say whiskey sour? I meant whiskey sours, and toasted each other on a great game, which we didn't have, and headed out to the Holley Inn. The waitress set two whiskey sours down in front of us. We looked at them, and she looked at us, and Gordon said, "I'm sorry. I think you made a mistake. I know we had a couple of drinks, but this is one we didn't order."

"Yes I know," she said, "but we have a rule here at the Holley Inn. When you drink a dozen, you get the 13th one free."

Our conversation turned to the Congressional hearings and the opening remarks that had been reported that day on "Payola in the Record Industry." As we stepped off the curb to cross the street from the Clubhouse, I said, "Gordon, there's gonna be big trouble."

He said, "Don't count your ugly chickens before they hatch."

That evening at dinner, I was called away from the table by the waiter to take a call. The General Manager of WBZ, Paul O'Friel, asked me if anyone had called me. He told me that seven disc jockeys had been featured as the Boston Globe's big story. I was not included because I was out of town. Boy, was I out of town, playing golf with a record distributor.

He said "Every Boston Newspaper has the payola investigation plastered all over the front page. If you are approached by any reporters, tell them that WBZ is the official spokesperson on this issue."

I went back to the table and told Gordon the goings on and he said, "Do you think they'll send a guy from Washington to my little storefront in Boston?"

It turned out that his instincts were right, but they didn't send one guy. . . . They sent three guys (investigators) from the Senate Investigative Subcommittee on Payola.

A couple of days later, I headed back to Boston and WBZ. I went on the air that afternoon. It was the strangest feeling to listen to the newsman as he did his newscast, and I'm the lead story.

Keep in mind, it was an election year and about a month later, I was gifted with a swell subpoena from the Congressional Sub-committee to appear and testify in Washington.

It was just like the movies. I was the first to testify before the Committee. I testified for four hours, and my testimony is all in the Congressional Record. They asked me if I accepted gifts, and I said *yes*, but only from the artists that I knew would have hits. I was called a "recalcitrant witness" by Rep. John Moss. He then asked me how I knew which records would be hits, and I told him that every Friday and Saturday night I held record hops, and at the end of each record I would ask the kids if they thought the song would be a hit.

When I was excused, I got my coat and started to walk out. I was grabbed by Mike San Angelo, Public Relations Director of Westinghouse (They owned WBZ at the time). I was in a daze. He grabbed my lapels and said, "You did good, kid. When you step out the exit door you will be besieged by movie cameras and I don't know how many microphones, and they'll all be looking for quotes. Screw 'em!"

I'd like to tell you a little bit about Mike San Angelo. He was a very creative guy and earlier in his career, was responsible for the publicity and public relations for a major soap advertiser. The advertiser decided to introduce a new soap product and decided to use New York City as a test market. Mike hired a hundred kids, or so, at $1.00 an hour, to walk up and down the streets of Manhattan and 5th Avenue and use the soap to write on *all* the windows they could with drawings, poetry, etc. to promote the new product. The windows, all got soaped and everybody was talking about it. It really was a great marketing idea.

Mike patted me on the back and through the exit door I went. Boy, what a mob. I made my way through that crowd, and stumbled down the sidewalk in a daze. I don't know how far I walked, but I did become aware that the cold February rain was soaking through my clothing. Although almost soaked to the skin, I stopped and bought a few papers on my way back to the hotel. I bought a Boston Globe, The NY Times, the St. Louis Post Dispatch, and the Chicago Tribune. I hailed a cab and said, "Mayflower Hotel."

As I approached my room, I thought, *Boy, would a martini hit the spot right now.*

As I opened the door, there was my wife, martinis in hand, God love her.

You know, it was really amazing. I spread the papers out on the floor and, my God, all five stories about the day's testimony were absolutely nothing alike.

For instance, my father called me on the telephone and said, "David, why would you wear a yellow sport jacket to court?"

I said, "Dad I don't even own a yellow sports jacket." What I wore was a button down oxford shirt, tie and tweed jacket.

The next morning, I went to the airport to board my flight. As I trudged up the gangway, a pretty little stewardess took one look at me and said, "Don't go back."

I asked, "Big headlines?"

She replied, "War type."

The following week, I got a call informing me that I was under suspension from the station with full pay.

After five weeks of doing nothing, I finally got a call telling me I was reinstated at WBZ.

Later that same day, I got a call from a reporter at the Record American. He called to let me know he had written an article to run in that evening's edition telling everyone that I was terminated from WBZ. He said, "You've been out for five weeks. That's kind of a long time to be sick."

"Well," I said, very blasé, "I'm going back to work this after-noon."

He said, "Good luck."

Boy, did I ever dodge that bullet.

Chapter 6

Traveling With Dave

As spokesman for Crimson Travel, I traveled once a year for 22 years with a tour group. I hope these stories encourage you to explore and enjoy the world and its ways, as I did. They are not in chronological order, but each story is memorable by itself.

Hong Kong

Style Man, Style

On a number of occasions, I've been called upon to rate the dramatic city of Hong Kong. It is undoubtedly an *ooh* and *ahh* delight. Needless to say, I was a little impressed when they rolled out our transportation for the trip to the hotel. As a matter-of-fact, I distinctly remember hearing my wife say, "You can really close your mouth now."

Not a bus . . . not a taxi . . . not a limousine, but there, parked at the curb in classic racing green, was a Silver Cloud Rolls Royce sedan – a beautiful car, and it was ours for the next few hours. Strange thing now, but if you've never ridden in a Rolls Royce, you'll find that you have a tendency to look down at people as you drive past. It could be worse, I suppose. You could stick your nose in the air as well. Just in case I forgot to mention it, the car was owned by a British concern, which also owned the hotel.

The Hong Kong Peninsula Hotel was run like an old-line British money hotel. Since the year I paid a visit to the Peninsula Hotel, the company bought some other properties. Lovely places, all with lots of old-world charm, but The Peninsula, after all, *is* The Peninsula. (In today's dollars, their minimum rate translates to about $600 per night, not bad for 1979.)

They didn't welcome large tourist groups, but fortunately, the fellow making our travel arrangements was related to the individual planning our stay in Hong Kong, so we lucked out and stayed at this grand hotel. Our group was around 60 people.

We had to tell everyone at the orientation meeting before we handed out everyone's room keys, "Do not steal the ashtrays."

They had big, beautiful ceramic ashtrays, and I told them, "Maybe it's funny now, but it won't be funny later if they catch you with one of their ashtrays!"

The hotel was beautiful – Top of the line, high class, with every accoutrement imaginable. I was delighted to see a gentleman, who was obviously a houseboy, smile and bow as I walked past him in the hallway. We actually had houseboys in the hallways, and they were there all night - ready, willing, and able to fulfill our every need and desire. So, if you wanted to order a martini at 4 a.m., he was there to get it for you!

We were there with our wives and enjoyed the "high-end service."

One of the things I always wanted to do was to have my clothing washed, dried and ironed by a Chinese laundry in Hong Kong, which, by the way, turned out to be ferociously expensive. I think a shirt, washed and ironed, same day service, was about $8.00. Incidentally, the hotel was right on the harbor, and the Hong Kong ferry slip was about 50 yards away. The cost for this refreshing and breezy 10 minute ride was three cents for a regular fare, and four cents for first class. Sure beats the deal on shirts.

One last thought: if you ever get to Hong Kong, there's a good chance that you'll be subject to a sales pitch like no other, having to do with a romantic, delicious dinner on a native sampan, right in Hong Kong harbor, serving tempura-style shrimp and various vegetables with three or four different appetizers, and to this day, I cannot tell you what they were. Wine was to be part of the meal, as well as potato somethings. It was really kind of picturesque. Hot oil bubbling with shrimp and pork somethings. It looked super. Unfortunately . . . it wasn't.

Most of vegetables were rotten, quite inedible. Bad food has a certain smell about it, and it's very hard to cover up. You couldn't wash it down with the wine because, although there was liquid in the wine bottle, after careful examination we realized the wine bottle had been carefully opened and recapped after the contents had been cut with water. So anyhow, if you run into this same situation, and you're tempted to try it, DON'T! Although to be frank, I'll bet food scams of this nature are now few and far between since Chairman Mao and his followers took over. I've heard many stories since the regime change making the point that everybody is now on their best behavior or they face dire consequences.

We decided to go to dinner with some friends at the Hotel. The couple we went to dinner with was the Chief Operating Officer of Standex, out of Derry, New Hampshire. His name was Warren Cooper and his wife was Joyce. They were close friends of ours, so we decided to dine together. I was going to mention, we were going Dutch, but I never got around to it. We ordered dinner, *à la carte* off the menu, including two bottles of wine, and then the bill came. I made a half-hearted grab for the bill, but Warren made even less of one. The bill was $456. Although the check was right in front of me, no one was making a move toward it. Never trust a zillionaire. I made a point of telling him it would take about nine different restaurants to make up for that dinner I had paid for. All things considered though, he was quite a generous man. Later, I signed a contract to do the radio and television advertising spots for his company.

Little Rock, AK - 1980s

It was 1980 and we decided we needed to visit a plant that produced one of the products Warren Cooper was managing for Standex. The plant was located in a small town outside of Little Rock, Arkansas. After we set the date and time of the two-day visit to Arkansas, I naturally assumed we would be flying first class. I was wrong. It was better than first class. They had their own jet.

We left on his corporate Cessna Citation that flew at 49,000 feet. Although the jet was like flying in someone's living room with lounge chairs, it lacked a private bathroom.

Warren's wife, Joyce, announced midway through the trip that she needed to use a bathroom, so Warren went up to the pilots and told them about the situation. The pilots then changed their flight plan to land in Knoxville, Tennessee, to accommodate her. We ended up purchasing sandwiches at a sandwich automat to bring back on the jet, as apparently there was no food on board, and then proceeded to our destination. On the way back home, we stopped at a Kentucky Fried Chicken to bring some with us on the plane. Even though the lush interior of the plane lacked food and bathroom facilities, it was stocked with a full bar. So, we had Kentucky Fried Chicken and two martinis on the way home. Needless to say, it turned out to be a very pleasant flight.

Warren was a very nice man and one of my best friends, and also very capable at *not* picking up dinner checks.

Morocco - Early 1970s

It was the early 1970s and boy, what a party, and of all places, in a bus. We left Casablanca just after lunch and kept going until we reached a modernized oasis. The oasis specialized in thirsty tourists, and had freshly squeezed orange juice for their patrons – a lot of it. I knew this beforehand so I had purchased some plastic containers, paper cups and vodka . . . lots of vodka . . . at least four liters. I then polled the lovely people on the bus. "Who wants a screwdriver?"

42 of the 45 said, "Yes!" We had two more hours to go to reach Marrakesh, and boy, did we enjoy the ride. We sang, had a joke contest, which by the way, everybody lost. The jokes were terrible, inasmuch as I was the only judge. Well, it worked out just fine, and we arrived late afternoon at La Mamounia Hotel in Marrakech, just in time for a nap.

What a successful trip. We spent four days there. Now, I've seen some beautiful hotel rooms, but I must admit that the riad (rooms)

my daughter, Marney and I were given, were as nice as it gets, and the accommodations, to put it in perspective, were the quintessential expression of discreet opulence, according to their brochure (It was amazing. You need to check this hotel out on the internet).

The riad included Aubusson rugs, unbelievably exquisite tile work, marble floors, *amazingly* spacious accommodations, with a balcony overlooking the gardens, freshly-cut flowers every day, a magnificent private pool, without a doubt, fit for a king. It was, after all, a former palace, so I was sure it had accommodated a king or two before we arrived. You can understand I wasn't shocked when the Assistant Manager of the Hotel told me how many members of royalty and statesmen had occupied our riad in the past. But, I was really impressed when he listed one of the most important men in the world. I speak of Sir Winston Churchill, as a previous occupant. Churchill loved to paint, especially when he visited La Mamounia Hotel and painted the lovely gardens from the 2nd floor balcony. We were now experiencing and enjoying a true bit of history.

I got a kick out of answering the knocks at my door from members of our tour group. Each time, they asked a special favor of me. They all wanted to know if it would be possible for them to come in and take of photo of the suite. And where do you think they wanted to pose? By the beautiful balcony overlooking the gardens? No. Or perhaps next to the exquisite tile work in the main living area of the suite? No. Next to the magnificent pool? No. It was the simple, but stunningly beautiful marble bathtub in our suite.

As I look back now, of the days spent in Marrakech, I would be remiss as a travel reporter if I did not recall for you, a rather unusual night. One of the members of our travel group was a 24-year-old beautiful blonde girl, with a very attractive way about her. Her name was Jewel . . . and that's the kind of girl she was. I was only mildly surprised when she told me she was approached by the maitre d'. He had proposed marriage to her.

I said, "Uh huh, and what did you say?"

She responded, "Oh, puleeze!"

I said, "All right, I'll speak to him and tell him you're not interested and you're not for sale." Oops, I forgot to tell you his offer included three cows, and I jokingly told him she couldn't go for less than four. I saw him again the next day, and I thanked him for being such a gentlemen.

However, my daughter, Marney, was upset. She said, "Dad, he only offered one cow for me."

From Russia With Love? - mid 1980s

To be truthful, I was more than mildly surprised at the number of people who were genuinely taken aback that I had chosen, of *all* places to visit, Russia. These were the same people who, every time they travel, pick an itinerary that provides for a stopover that would include at least one day at the beach. Needless to say, you're not ever going to find a good beach day in Russia, plus the fact that you would have to travel all the way down to Odessa to find a place to swim.

It was the mid 1980s and we were the first tour group to visit Russia at the end of the Cold War. We flew from New York and landed in Oslo, Norway, where we spent two days looking around. Looking around must include a visit to The Vigeland Sculpture Park. It is very popular, but don't go. if you have *any* aversion to sex. This monolith (left), representing all of humanity, is the centerpiece of the Vigeland Sculpture Park.

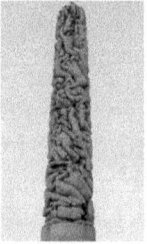

Next we went from Oslo to Sweden on an overnight ferry. Nobody goes to bed, to go to sleep that is. We just danced the night away. A couple of days in Sweden, and it was on to Helsinki, Finland where, among other things, we enjoyed the bathtub ritual. The ritual entails the use of long-handled soft brushes to scrub the person in front of you, eventually forming a circle of scrubbers. A lot of laughing goes on. I managed to include myself into several of these brush-baths. I had a smile on my face for six days.

Finally, we arrived in Leningrad. This was one of the main reason I chose to visit Russia. Our hotel was one of the big old ones, and my suite was quite historic, with a view of the Neva River. The room was both spacious and regal, with a magnificent grand piano and a marble bath tub. Across the inlet was the view of the light battleship, Aurora.

One of the most impressive sights in Leningrad is the Memorial commemorating the Great Siege of Leningrad, with twin mounds of earth, about 100 feet square. Each mound contained 2,000 bodies, one mound of 2,000 civilians and the second with 2,000 soldiers.

There was quiet music in the background, playing continuous Russian war songs emanating from a Gazebo between the two mounds. As visitors entered the gazebo, they would view a whole series of large photographs depicting the siege.

One look at the plane that was to fly us to Moscow and, I thought, *Gee, I wish I could hitchhike.* It was a twin engine jet aircraft with chipped paint, various dents and engines, which I swear to God, coughed. Now I *really* wished I could hitchhike. We all had boarding passes, but no seat assignments. One lucky break – there were about 10 of us from our group who were kind of clumped together. This was lucky, because one person had a liter of vodka, and we all wanted to have one shot, before the plane took off. One problem . . . no glass. The flight attendant was almost six feet tall, and weighed about 190 lbs. We got her attention and asked for a glass. I will never forget watching the woman stride toward us with a glass in one hand, and her dirty apron in the other. She used the apron to wipe the glass and then blew into it. She spoke not one word of English. What the Hell. We didn't want to hear very much from her anyway. You'll be interested to know the plane made it, and, with the help of Smirnoff, we did too.

When we arrived at our hotel and, checked in, and as is so typical of Russian hotel life, not only were there no suites with a piano, but our beds were all singles that you pulled out of the wall, like a very large drawer. We were then told to assemble in the lobby, where we were to be given a lecture on the rules and regulations of the hotel, and also what we would be doing for the next three days. One good thing, our hotel was only four blocks from Red Square, and that's what I came to see. Just around the corner, within walking distance from our hotel, was St. Basil's Cathedral, Lenin's Tomb, the Gum Department Store, and, of course, the formidable Kremlin Wall.

The next day, when we came down for breakfast, the waitress came and put a bottle of soda of some sort on our table. After another 15 minutes came a cup of coffee. I think it was coffee, and a plate for everyone to share. The plate had on it a large round piece of mystery meat and one fried egg for each person. Not very much of this was partaken. The waitress looked at us rather disdainfully, but it couldn't match the look on the American faces when we were all told that breakfast was over. Everybody got up to leave and watched as the waitress cleared the tables, walked over to a wooden bureau, pulled out the drawer, and slid the uneaten eggs and meat into the drawer. One woman who was traveling with the group said in a low undertone, "I've got a funny feeling that's lunch." Now that I think it over, there was nothing funny about it at all.

Out we went on our way to Red Square. I couldn't help but notice something was different, and it took a couple of blocks before it hit me. You could pick out who was Russian, and who were the tourists because – and perhaps time has altered the habit – the Russians didn't look up when they walked. They stared at the sidewalk and made no eye contact. Whoever heard of a thing like that?

Once inside the Kremlin, we had to be very cautious and careful because the police whistle brigade were everywhere . . . very busy making sure everyone stayed inside the lines. What lines? you ask. Why the lines they painted every night. Step over the line and you've got a whistle in your face, and a nasty glare to go with it from the police. I inadvertently broke the rules by stepping over the yellow line. I really didn't step over the yellow line, I stepped on it, and for that I got a whistle, a glare, and a thumb wave. I thought to myself, *Boy, I'm really glad I didn't have both feet over the line* as there was no doubt in my mind the firing squad would be next. I guess there are troubles there we wouldn't dream of. As a matter of fact, it wasn't more than two weeks after we got home that two ladies were slaughtered in front of our very own hotel. I wondered if they were looking down every time they went out for a walk.

One night we were invited to a dinner dance at our hotel. After dinner, all the tables were cleared, a big band, 14 pieces or so, came in and set up. I was pleasantly surprised and knew we hit onto something good, because they opened up with Glenn Miller's *In the Mood*. When we got back to our tables, surprise number two; vodka, and the first drink was on the house. Smart move. An older lady in our group said, "How did they find out about us?"

I noticed as the evening progressed, that one of the saxophonists kept smiling at me. I mean one of those big, dazzling smiles . . . a come-hither smile, and I thought, *What the Hell is going on here?* Then came the band break, and he came right up to our table and introduced himself. I thought I'd pass out when he said in halting English, "May I talk to you for a minute?" He, by the way, was the first Russian to speak to me directly. He then said, "I can't speak to you for very long, but would it be possible for you to get me a new reed for my saxophone?"

At first I had a mild urge to laugh, but then I saw how serious he was, so I said, "Yes, I'll try."

He wanted a certain kind of reed, but couldn't give me his address, as people there were watching. His address would be delivered to me at the hotel the next day.

Three or four people who were traveling with me ended up sitting up with me most of that night. They swore they saw a man at the hotel tailing us, both in Leningrad and now in Moscow. They all had their theories, but on this, they were all in agreement. This same man, they had noticed in Leningrad had been shadowing us since we landed there and for our entire trip.

The next day, the address was delivered to the front desk, thank God, and, *Yes, I looked both ways leaving the hotel.*

Later, I did manage to find the requested reed on a stop-over on our trip back to the States, and sent it on its way to the smiling saxophonist.

By this time on our trip, you might wonder if there was a chance of starvation. Not me, kid. You're taking to *the* Jack Armstrong, the All-American Boy. That very afternoon, I entered a Russian salami store, where I saw quite a number of people standing in lines before the counter. Nobody spoke any English so, clever me, I pointed at some meat and the butcher said something in Russian and luckily, pointed to one of the three lines, followed by a wave of his hand. Even I could tell that meant, get to the back of the line, so I did. Now get this, if you ever intend to go to Russia anytime soon, I want you to keep in mind that I have trail blazed the way to shop for food, or anything else for that matter.

Here's how it's done. First, you get to the end of the first line, wait your turn, and order your merchandise. The man behind the counter then gives you a chit. Then you walk to the end of the second line, wait your turn again, where they prepare and package your merchandise. Then you walk to the end of the third line, hand over your chit and they give you your purchase. Above all, do not try to understand what you're supposed to be doing, and *smile, darn you, smile.*

You might be wondering a couple of things. First, how did the salami taste? Not bad, if you wash it down with vodka. Second, how does the butcher know how much salami you want to buy?

You had to gesture with your thumb and forefinger to show him how much you want. That's how you measure salami in Russia.

Now, I've already told you how the Russians handle salami buying. Here's another example of Russian hospitality. We all know, I'm sure, about the room service cards that are made available to the hotel guests. I picked up the card in my room, and started to peruse it. I couldn't quite understand what my room card was all about because someone had taken a pen and meticulously drawn a line through every available service listed. The card read: no room service, no valet, no concierge; In short, . . . no nothing.

I asked a friend of mine, who had spent a lot of time in Russia, "What the Hell does this mean?"

He said, "It means you're in Russia, and they like to see everyone working. It was someone's job to ink out that hotel room service card information."

I said, "Do grownup people really do this for a living? If so, I have a suggestion. Take the card away." We laughed at that for some time.

Here's another example of the strange ways that Russians handle situations. Coming back to my room one day, I noticed a man in the hallway. I nodded my head to him and said *hello*, and he nodded back but didn't say anything. However, I got a good look at him, and thought, *his face looks familiar, as it should, since he had been the fellow everyone in my tour group insisted had been trailing us since we arrived in Europe.*

By this time, with all the experiences we had with being watched and followed, I was firmly convinced that I was now the reincarnation of British Secret Agent James Bond, AKA 007.

When we got to Denmark, that was our next stop on the trip home, I kind of missed that familiar looking fellow. Everything turned out all right, but I still kept looking all over and everywhere in Copenhagen for him, but no dice. I guessed he was out buying sex magazines. I know I was.

So far I've spent a great deal of time telling you about the inequities in the USSR. Now let me tell you about something that was super-duper. A wonderful Russian circus that's held indoors in a round amphitheater that holds about 10,000 people, maybe more.

On the ground floor there was a complete collection of live farm animals, including ducks, chickens, small dogs, ponies, pigs, birds and goats. You get the sense that something is missing, for there were no people, except for the ringmaster, who left the stage as soon as the show began.

Narration was done by loud speaker in Russian. Ten minutes after we got there, the show began. The announcer started, and it was obvious that he was describing the set and the animals that were there, and what part they were playing in the performance . . . and what a performance.

First, one by one, the animals were introduced to the audience. So help me God, I thought some of the animals were mechanical. I mean even as smart as pigs are, when introduced, if you could believe it, the two pigs stepped forward two steps, and then stepped back in place.

Next came the fire scene. Now, keep in mind that all the animals I'm talking about take all their cues from the narrator, who is not even seen. Next up, the duck. He was in the farmhouse barn, up in the hayloft. He started bellowing, and why not, since the smoke poured out of the loft. DANGER . . . DANGER! I swear you felt it was like a human being crying, *Save Me. Save me!* Suddenly, from around the corner came the pony-drawn fire engine and animal fire brigade and boy, did they ring that bell. Slowly but surely, the animals did their jobs beautifully, and put the fire out. Get this; some of the animals fed the other animals as they performed their jobs. I guess the fire had interrupted their dinner time. In the finale, the ringmaster brought the house down, and guess how he did it – by simply walking off the stage. All the animals followed him. He was the boss all right.

I must admit, everybody was in a pretty good mood on our last night in Moscow. We were to be taken to the snazziest supper club in town, according to our guide. As we filed into the club the *ooo*s and *ahhh*s could be heard for miles. The table setting alone was gorgeous, with six beautiful crystal stemware goblets per setting. The next largest for the champagne, then the next for red wine, the next for white wine, and the next smallest for brandy, with the smallest for cognac. The largest was for water and, unfortunately, that was the only thing that tasted good. Then came the food . . . and we sent it all back.

Believe me friends, we had a discussion on how we were going to eat the food once we were served. Well, we reasoned, we can be fairly sure of one thing – that some of it was bound to be edible. We decided to just pick out our favorite dish from the menu, if there were such a thing, and share and share alike.

We ordered our choices and the waiter came back with whatever the chef decided he wanted to give us. What service! We had one ace in the hole, and that was the bread. We ordered more bread, and more bread after that. Oh, I almost forgot, shame on me, there was one other course which I was pretty sure would go over big, the vodka course. The course began when you picked up your first fork and ended when you left the table. Am I exaggerating? Well maybe just a little. (Note to the reader: Don't go to Russia for the food!)

A lot of thoughts ran through my mind as I sat there, inside the SAS jetliner, waiting for the engines to fire up for the flight home. I thought of the Russian folks I had met; the saxophone player, the waitresses in the dining room of our hotel, a maybe KGB shadow man, the security men who were all over the place walking out into Red Square, the salami salesmen on Gorky Street. All of a sudden I was, jolted out of my reverie as the DC-9 started to thunder down the runway. Then, all of a sudden, it's up, up and away! Quite a number of passengers cheered at the very moment the rear wheels left the ground. A bit later I asked my flight attendant, excuse me, they were called stewardesses back in the 1980s, "Does that applause happen often? The cheering, I mean."

She smiled and said, "Every time we leave the ground."

Just one final thought. I wanted to share with you, for your amusement, the following comments from a fellow traveler to Russia.

"The first thing I did when I returned to the free world after two weeks in Russia was to find a water cooler and drink heartily from it. I never located a single water cooler in the Soviet Union during my visit.

"After that, I found myself a restroom. I'm not certain of the figures, but I would guess there is something like one public restroom for every 250,000 citizens in the Soviet Union, and none have toilet paper. You show me a country short on toilets, and with no toilet paper for the public, and I will show you a country that is still a long way from world domination.

"There was toilet paper in my hotel rooms in the Soviet Union, but you can't just sit in your hotel room clinging to your toilet paper like a security blanket. You actually have to go outside some time and even if you take some of the hotel toilet paper with you, comfort is still not guaranteed.

"The Soviets make toilet paper, paper cups and ice cream cones from the same grade of paper. Coffee drips through the bottom of the cup in about 13 seconds. Soviet ice cream cones taste like the sports section, and a person could so severely injure himself with extended use of Soviet toilet paper that all the Preparation H on earth wouldn't help.

"The Soviet Union doesn't work.

"I plan to sit around for a couple of weeks squeezing the Charmin. God Bless America!"

These comments were written by Lewis Grizzard of *The Atlanta Journal,* September 1, 1985.

And now you know why I called this chapter, "From Russia With Love?"

KENYA - Early 1980s

It was the early 1980s. I was told by my wife that she was going to take me to Africa - East Africa to be exact. Kenya to be more exact. Little Governor's Camp, to be still more exact, right on the Serengeti Plain.

The first thing I did was to buy one of those safari outfits with all those patch pockets, and, of course, a hat. You have to have a safari hat. Then a trip to the mirror, and I could see in an instant that I wasn't going to look like Stuart Granger. Desert boots are a must, and overall, I looked not too bad, not too bad at all. Driving down a paved road toward Nairobi, we saw a Masai warrior. You couldn't miss him. He was six feet tall, leaner than sin, and carry-ing a heavy iron spear with a blunt end. He was bare-footed, walking on the pavement and he too, was headed toward Nairobi. As we passed him he looked straight ahead and paid no attention to us. We didn't do anything except gawk in awe. A Masai warrior be-comes a man once he has slain a lion with his spear.

There were nine in our little safari group, all New

Englanders. I was really happy to see that everybody had a neat sense of humor. On the DC-3 flight from Nairobi to the Little Governor's Camp, someone said to me, "Do you know what they call this aircraft once we get into the air? The Vomit Comet."

The airfield was a strip of tar. The hanger and the airport offices were nowhere to be seen, because there weren't any. Occasionally some people were sent out to walk the airstrip to shoo away nosey elephants. Now get this. The elephant goes wherever he wants to go, whenever he wants to go. The only deterrent that any of the camp directors used were two branches of a certain tree, that they would polish, and then smack them together, and for some reason, the elephants would retreat from that particular sound, but not in any hurry - you know, leisurely.

We stopped for lunch at a two-story restaurant on the road to Nairobi from the airport. We were seated on the second floor. Each table was situated next to a window. We could see giraffes approaching. Sur-prise, surprise. Giraffes have one of the longest tongues in the animal kingdom. Their tongues have some sort of sticky substance on it. That is when we found out why this restaurant was so popular with the local giraffes. They came over to our win-dow and stuck their head in, clamped the food onto their tongue and chewed away to their heart's content, while all the tourists go hungry.

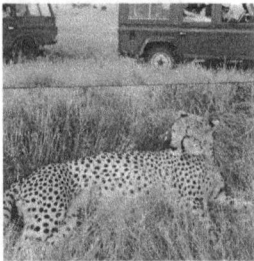

We had our own Land Rover and drove out to our Little Governor's Camp. When you go on safari in Africa, you travel in Land Rovers to facilitate animal spotting.

The guide had taken an acetylene torch and cut the top off the vehicle, so that people could stand up and get the best view possible. Each person, of course, reported to our guide, Faread, and driver, Jackson, and alerted everybody to an animal sighting.

I can't believe how close we came to those magnificent wild animals. In some cases we drove to within 40 or 50 feet of them. A mistake you don't want to make is to drive too close to a pride of lions that haven't eaten in some time. Almost all the animals roam freely and, because there

are no gunshots, they don't run in panic. For the most part humans are given great leeway by the animals.

Now let's talk about the animals. What your guide pretty much guarantees you is getting fairly close to the *Big Five*. The *Big Five* consists of lion, leopard, rhinoceros, hippopotamus, and water buffalo.

Water buffalo may surprise you until you come upon a patch of them, and they slowly turn towards you. Their antlers are deadly. They sharpen them every day on trees, and will charge any animal unprovoked. I was told by our guide, Faread, that he had taken a party out on the afternoon run. By the way, there were three photo safaris every day, one at 6:30 a.m., one at 12:30 p.m., and one at 4:30 p.m.

Well, anyhow, there was a member of one party who was a big drinker, but not a particularly wise drinker. After lunch at which he consumed multiple martinis, he did something everyone was warned about, time and again: "Don't wander off."

Big drinker wandered off. By the time his absence was noticed and a search party sent out, it was about 1:30 p.m. When they finally found him, he obviously had been attacked by a water buffalo with those huge sharp horns. He had been gored several times.

It has been said that there is a certain M.O. to a water buffalo attack, which includes goring the victim and throwing him up a tree. It was obvious that he had been done-in by a water buffalo.

Another member of the *Big Five* is the one who goes up the tree, where the water buffalo has thrown its prey - the leopard. The leopard is a very smart animal. He will eat in the tree, if there is too much going on at ground level.

Hold on, I forgot something. I forgot to include potentially the most dangerous of all in the *Big Five* list and I need to add it to the list to become *The Big Six*. It's the very same animal who loves to scratch his body on the straw houses at all safari camps, or on any handy tree - the elephant.

Several times during our stay at the camp, an elephant (or several elephants) would leisurely stroll into our compound, on the same path we often took, sort of checking us out. On the day we were leaving, I had stopped to tie my shoe, and all of a sudden my wife said, "Look."

I stood up, and turned around. Before I could say anything, my wife made a statement I will never forget. She said, "Elephant!" That's all she needed to say, just that: "Elephant," and lo and behold, he stopped in his tracks. We, on the other hand, did not stop in our tracks. We hightailed it around behind our sleeping quarters. Oh, by the way, I forgot to mention, our sleeping quarters were tents. We knew one thing. If an elephant wants to hurt you, there's no stopping him.

Perhaps you're wondering about safety and why, for instance, the safaris don't have guns. Most of the animals have no fear of people because people are not considered a threat to their well-being. Of course, poachers are another story entirely.

Okay, let's go ballooning. Our day started first with a light breakfast, not meant to weigh you down. A pot of tea and a couple of digestive cookies (made with oatmeal). Then it's on to the ballooning field.

What a sight it was. There were 3 balloons, just about all fired up. Nine of us jumped into one. When that Balloon Master says, "Go," you go . . . or you miss the balloon. We all made it on board, and up we went.

Quiet. That's what it was . . . quiet. The only noise was made by the furnaces that fired the balloons with hot air. Our Balloon Master was a real cornball. He was six feet tall, a big shock of brown hair, and a great British accent. He was, handsome. I hated him. Now get this. We came out over the tree line, right next to the biggest flowering tree below, and Mr. Cornball leaned over and plucked a blossom, which he presented with great flourish to one of the ladies in our group. I made the suggestion, inasmuch as there were four ladies in our group, that he jump out of the balloon and pick three more blossoms, but he pointed out, very quickly, that there would then be no one to run the balloon. See why I hated him?

As we ascended, we all were aware of a great deal of thrashing under our balloon. It was a pretty scary sound coming from a herd of elephants below. The elephants were panicked by the sound of the furnaces firing the balloon upward, which gave off quite a roar. Elephants can't look upwards, above a certain height, and only knew they were afraid of the sound.

Now, once again, the quiet of the Serengeti Plain. Oh, I neglected to tell you why the balloons left at 5:30 in the morning. It's quite a thrill to look eastwardly and see the sunrise over the Serengeti, and to see the number of animals roaming the Plain. It was really something as light broke. We saw zebras, wildebeest, lions, gazelles and giraffes.

It was about 7:30 a.m., and I'll tell you, I'm a breakfast fan. We started to descend. It took us about 25 minutes to land and my stomach was really growling by then. I had noticed three pick-up trucks that had followed our path as we traveled. The men in the trucks had stopped, deflated the balloons and rolled them up on the ground. After all, we had to have something to rest our backs on while we were being served breakfast.

It was rather nice, don't you think, to immediately be served a mimosa. Nothing like chilled champagne when you're on the Serengeti Plain. Then came the plates of fluffy yellow scrambled eggs, a whole bunch of sautéed mushrooms, and rich, dark coffee . . . a breakfast feast. Oh, by the way, we couldn't help but notice that about 50 yards from our breakfast was a huge lion, who was chewing on a freshly killed impala.

If East Africa is going to be part of your travel plans, do try to include William Holden's Resort now known as The Fairmont Mount Kenya Safari Club. The Nanyuki Retreat is located in Nanyuki, Kenya, for a number of reasons. Situated some one hundred and ninety kilometers north of Nairobi on the slopes of Mount Kenya, it has a reputation for relaxed elegance. Many of the world's most famous names, be they royalty, film stars, or merely the rich, seek it out as a secluded haven where, although you wear your safari gear during the day, you always *dress* for dinner. Sir Winston Churchill was reputed to have been a founding member. The food was well-prepared and the service impeccable. They poured a mean drink, the accommodations were handsome, and they had a golf course.

What a golf course it was. It was a little different from other golf courses. You rent the golf balls. They do remind you that if you hit a ball into the bush, (We call it the woods here in the U.S.) don't go and look for it. There are several species of things that slide in the bush, as well as bite. We weren't playing very well, so we made up another game to play. We called it, *Find That Turd*. For some reason, some of the animals prefer defecating on the fairways. What's so provocative was that they have God knows how many shapes and forms; the Curlicues, Torpedoes, Cherry Bombs, Mammoths, and Flops, and probably a couple more that I can't think of. Don't get nervous. The game did not include hitting the turd with a golf club.

Another thing you must do is buy some of the hand-made native straw and leather bags. On our last day there, we were told that we could get great buys on the best bags made. Jackson, our driver, took us outside the Nairobi city walls to a local market. It was there that we met a group of middle-aged ladies who, quite frankly, looked as though they needed the business. They looked to be dressed in rags, and we were told by our hotel staffer, that we should bargain. I had a tough time with my high school French, and wasn't sure that this Arab lady wasn't going to take advantage of me. By the way, I don't speak Arabic. I turned to Jackson and asked him to translate, and he said, "Sure, except for one thing; you had better buy from these ladies, and points to a group sitting together on the ground . . . or he'll (Faread) kill me! It turned out he was related to the ladies dressed in rags.

One woman stood up and quoted me a price on a bag. I think it was $15.

"No," I said, "that's too much."

She spoke to Jackson and he said to me, "These bags are all hand-made."

I then told him, "They are beautiful bags, but I want your lowest price now, because I haven't got much time. I'll pay you $5 a bag."

She replied, "No, that's not enough."

I then told her I wanted 56 bags, and my offer of $5 per bag was one-time only. Boy, was I puffed up with my negotiating skills.

She fished into her rag clothing, all the while talking a mile a minute to Jackson, and pulled out a calculator. A calculator mind you, dressed in all those rags, and after doing some math said, "Sold!"

We still have our beautiful hand-made bag today, nearly 30 years later. By the way, I found out later that good old Jackson was getting a kickback on my purchases from that lady dressed in rags.

On the last day of our stay at Governor's Camp, I was asked by Faread if I had seen enough animals.

I said, "Well, to tell you the truth, I did want to see a pack of wild dogs." Wild Africa dogs are not hyenas. They're something else entirely.

Wild East African dogs are funny looking dogs with Mickey Mouse ears and about the size of a Springer spaniel, but there the comparison ends. These wild dogs are killers, and this will make you wince; it is not unusual to see them hunt in large packs, sometimes as many as 30. Because of their size, they attack from the rear. My guide said, "You can always tell a kill in progress by the terrible shrieks of pain from their prey, because they have to kill in small bites."

Faread said, "Do you still want to go and see wild dogs?"

I said, "Yes." So we hopped into the Land Rover and drove about five miles.

We spotted a pack and what a shock. There were about 50 to 60 wild dogs and they were rolling around on their backs and happy and frolicking around. I was actually kind of relieved that we didn't see some kind of prey being chewed from the ass forward.

Then we took off for camp. We were traveling along at a pretty good clip when we suddenly came to a screeching halt, right under a huge fig tree. Faread pointed up and said, "Look up in the tree."

There sat one of the largest baboons I had ever seen glaring at us. Our guide said, "We're not going to spend a large amount of time here. We've interrupted him. He's busy gathering figs for his family and doesn't want us here. He's going to do everything possible to scare us away."

What an act! He first yawned to show us his teeth. He beat his chest along with emitting many snarls, and I must admit, I was getting pretty uncomfortable.

Then somebody in the Rover said, "Uh oh," because from between the baboon's legs a large phallus started to appear. He grabbed it with both hands, and one of the guys in our Land Rover said - and I will never forget it, "You'll Go Blind!"

We left. Back to the camp. We had packing to do, and even though we had very little time, we squeezed in another sighting of Hippopotami.

The next day we boarded the *"vomit"* Comet and flew to Nairobi, and guess what? When we got there, we were greeted with the news that we missed our connecting plane.

The pilots had gotten drunk the night before and didn't show up.

Our tour guide, Cynthia, managed to convince a bush pilot to fly all of us to Nairobi. Now, to be truthful, I don't relish taking off late in the afternoon in a single engine Piper with seating for eight; there were nine of us. All I could think of is that I'm flying in a blivit. (A blivit, for those not familiar with the term, is two pounds of shit in a one-pound bag). One thing more, I was reading a brochure for people who fly in and out of Mombasa that indicated they flew at 9,000 feet.

I yelled up to Cynthia and said, "Do me a favor will you? Read me the altimeter."

She responded, "8,000 feet."

I asked her to please ask him to fly 1,000 feet higher. How we made it to Nairobi, I don't know. We caught our connecting flight with 15 minutes to spare.

Cruise on the Delta Queen

Short But Sweet!

Having a mint julep is something; having four mint juleps is

really something; never mind five. We were on the Delta Queen, a paddleboat steamer, heading up the Mississippi to Natchez. It was the afternoon of the Kentucky Derby, and we celebrated big time. It was Churchill Downs on the water. The drinks were two for one for mint juleps, and we all were enthralled with the music as the

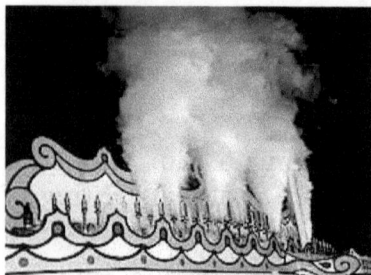

steam calliope was going full blast playing, *Waiting For the Robert E. Lee.* Let me tell you, brother, when they say steam calliope they really mean it. I'd never seen one before, and it was a source of delight. When the calliope player sat down and hit a four-tone cord, I was hooked. I was the closest to the calliope, and believe it or not, I was getting soaked . . . but who cares. Give me another mint julep.

Bull Fighting in Spain

See It Before It Is Banned - if you can take it!

I have only been to Spain once, and I made a promise to myself to go back again, because there's still an awful lot to see, not the least of which is Ferdinand. Ferdinand? Yes, you know, Ferdinand, the Bull. He's the one who sat under the cork tree. Now isn't that something? He certainly wasn't where he should have been while all the other young bulls were in a bullring practicing lunging and spearing with their horns. Ferdinand was sitting under a cork tree. In a way it's kind of painful to think about Ferdinand, because his future is awfully glum. There will come a time in his life when he'll be transported to the *Plaza de Toros* in Madrid, which is the scene of much carnage. The *Banderilleros* see to that.

They enter the arena after the Picadors (who arrive on horseback) have taken several swipes at the bull with their lances to weaken him. Three *Banderilleros* then enter carrying two *banderillas* each. These are decorated sharp, barbed sticks that they attempt to plant into the bull's shoulders to further weaken him. The desired result is to weaken the bull enough that his head will lower and his speed will be slower. After that, the Matador, with his cape and sword enters the arena to do his job. His job, of course, is to taunt the bull into his final charges, and deliver his demise with a precision thrust of his sword.

Every Sunday, in the *Plaza de Toros*, six bulls are brought into the arena to entertain the masses. A typical day at the arena is six hours or so, since each fight is broken down into three 20 minute segments. It was quite a sight to see, as I sat there waiting for the bull to arrive . . . and he did. His entrance is preceded by complete silence and then . . . the gate opens and *Tah Daah* . . . the bull enters amidst the blare of coronets and a shrieking frenzy of blood-thirsty spectators.

CESAR MANSO/AFP/Getty Images

Meanwhile, Ferdinand is still sitting under the cork tree, oblivious to it all.

The Matador has proceeded to the center of the arena, where he is first assisted with the removal of his ornate, skin tight jacket. Cheers explode as he receives the weapon and cape, and the ritual begins.

First, the bull stands in the center of the ring as the toreadors work to distract the bull to keep him active. He has lost a lot of blood, which of course, has weakened him, and his mighty neck is now bowed and bloody.

Meanwhile, the Matador has been watching. It's important for him to thrust his sword at just the right moment. The crowd signals the Matador when the time has come to slay the bull by shouting, over and over again, "Ole, Ole!" in unison. If he thrusts at just the right moment the bull dies, and the crowd roars.

If he takes too long to kill the bull, the crowd roars again, and in some cases (after all, the bull has taken a lot of punishment), they bring out a special killing sword. The sword is razor sharp, a T-shaped instrument of death, that in one stroke, severs the spinal cord, and the bull dies instantly. The wildly excited group expresses displeasure with this kind of death by tossing their seat cushions onto the floor of the arena, but . . . no matter, there are five more bulls to go.

The bull's carcass is then dragged off the arena floor by work horses, and later delivered to charitable institutions and orphanages for their consumption. You figure six bulls weighing approximately 700 pounds each, that's a lot of beef for a lot of people.

I've got something that should gladden your heart a little bit. During the very first appearance of the first bull of the day, the picador's mail-clad horse was knocked down by the bull. Our tour group of 60 went crazy. Crazy for the bull, not for the horse. We all leapt to our feet, and cheered like crazy for the bull. We looked around us and saw a sea of hate, and remember, there were only 60 of us, and a couple of thousand rabid Spaniards with mean looks on their faces. One lady in our group got hit with a flying seat cushion. We all sat down very quickly.

If you're fascinated and you would like to try bullfighting yourself, there are several bullfighting arenas and several places where you can take lessons and learn to fight bulls without getting too many holes in your clothes.

Just about everyone in our tour group was having a grand time. All except Gregory, a 34 year old, who as the Irish say, "Always had an elbow of an ass." On our final day, we were approached by the head honcho of the toreadors. He asked us if anyone was interested in trying their luck in the arena with a bull. One couple said they'd like to try it, and then another couple decided they'd like to try it as well, so off we went.

I was the first person selected to fight a bull. Gregory wanted to try it too, and I wasted no time squashing his desire. "Look, Gregory," I said, "it's not a very smart thing for you to do this. After all, you haven't gotten over your broken ankle yet, not to mention your broken hip. These are all young bulls - faster than the full grown ones, and oh, surfeit it to say, it's too dangerous for you. Tyrone Power did this great in the movies, but you're not Tyrone Power."

Gregory replied, "If an old man like you can do it, I can do it."

By the way, I was 37 years old at the time.

I was pretty nervous as I stepped into the center of the ring, but I must admit I was kind of thrilled at the same time. As I entered, although there wasn't an orchestra heralding my appearance, there was a band that was playing one of the best pieces of music I'd ever heard. It was music to my ears. Be prepared to be startled, as when I'd done two or three passes with the bull, I was amazed at my facial sneers as I tried to stare him down.

As soon as the bull blasted past the cape, I had to flip around to face him again. I had to be quick on my feet as the young bull was very quick on his. Fortunately, I had my dancing shoes on, but unfortunately for Gregory, he did not.

As I look back on the experience, I can truthfully say the word that best describes my feeling – and that word was **Dread.**

Gregory was up next. I was ready to run back into the arena . . . to do what? l don't know.

Into the ring limped Gregory to face his bull. I will say that even with his limp, he looked pretty positive as he strolled toward the bull. The bull then added his own drama to the scene. With everybody watching, he started pawing at the ground with his hooves, and then added a very loud and recognizable snort. El Toro obviously did not want this to drag on, and started his thrust almost immediately. I noticed in horror that he was not charging toward the cape that Gregory had extended to the left of his body. Instead, his charge was aimed straight at Gregory. It was obvious right away that he was going to be hit, and hit he was. A loud shriek of anticipation by the crowd let everybody know what agony we were all going through, which worsened as each millisecond passed. I forgot to mention that in the ring as well, were two or three handlers, former matadors, and wise in the ways of the bullring. It was a very good thing they were there. Their job was obvious, to draw off the bull, which they did, but not soon enough. Not soon enough to prevent Gregory from flying over the bull's horns. Thank God, and lucky for Gregory, there was a hospital nearby. When we spoke to the doctors on duty, they stressed, in no uncertain terms, that he was a lucky man.

Well, let's see. How lucky is lucky? Gregory's spleen was ruptured. His pelvis was broken, as were several ribs. He was put in a full body cast which doubled his normal weight. In fact his total weight was about 350 pounds, and he was now looking at months and months of rehab.

If this is what they call good luck in the hospitals of Spain, should I ever get the chance to visit again, I'm sure gonna load up my suitcase with as many good luck charms as I can carry.

Splendid China

I started to think about traveling to China somewhere in the late 1970s, and was told many times not to waste my time. It was too dangerous to travel to China. Then in the late 1970s, we entered a period of detente, and finally on a beautiful summer day in May of 1979, I received a telephone call. Oh, how well I remember that. It was my travel people informing me that, like a bolt out of the blue, the Chinese government had okayed 35 visas.

My response was, "Any chance of getting visas for 70 because there are 35 people who want to go already."

I mean, I don't want to be a piggy and we were the very first tour group to be allowed to visit China, but so many people wanted to experience traveling to this mysterious country, that they had thrown caution to the winds and signed up to spend close to

$2,000 apiece. Months later, as I stood there in the middle of Tiananmen Square, and did a complete turnaround, I was so thrilled that I wished I had brought a thousand people with me.

I learned a lot of things on this first trip to China. You will see in these pages the phrase, *In China we have a way of doing things*. It was proved to us all wide-eyed American travelers that they really *do* have a way of doing things.

I suppose anybody who travels, learns that when you are told the best way to do something (whether you're traveling to China,

Germany or Timbuktu), it is wisest to do it their way. You will do a lot better, and it will turn out to be nicer, if your conduct conforms to their way of doing things.

We were met at the airport by a gentlemen, middle-aged, who obviously was *Mr. Big.* The way the tourist groups would be handled by the Chinese Travel Bureau was very, very simple. He was there to welcome us, and it was obvious from his remarks, that we would have a good time if we obeyed the rules. He made it quite clear that we were, "Not to give thank-you gifts or presents, no gratuity, no nothing to our tour guides."

I was a jogger in that phase of my life, so when one of my traveling companions announced at the dinner table that she would jump at the chance to jog with a generous handful of Chinese runners, I said "fine."

That was before I was aware that the runners convened at 4:30 a.m. in the Square.

Then there were the calisthenics after we had jogged, and as I grunted and groaned my way through the regimen, I had visions of the front page of the Boston Globe: "Radio Personality Drops Dead in Tiananmen Square."

One of the things that really knocked me out was the age of the people running, roughly ages 8 to 78, and how many people practiced Tai Chi in the morning . . . almost everybody. Waiting for a bus or trolley, one can definitely get a little exercise just about anyplace. Where there is room to move around a little bit, you can get in a little exercise.

On the last morning of this killer exercise, I can't begin to tell you how much scraping and bowing was going on. Through my translator, I thanked the running group, and their very capable trainer for allowing us to work out with them.

He responded, "Thank you for giving me the honor. We have much to learn from each other, and also the highlight of our mornings together was that we have come to admire greatly your running suits."

I started to laugh. I couldn't help it. I was taken aback that he was so impressed with our exercise outfits.

Later on, we went into Shanghai. Everybody wanted to shop, and the Chinese make it as easy as possible to do so. At last count, there

were, I believe, 16 department stores. How do you know your way around to the different stores? you ask. Easy. Find out the number of the department store and tell the taxi driver which number store you want (for example, #11, #8).

Something fascinating. We watched from our cab as we traveled from one store to another in a big traffic jam. But not your typical traffic jam at all! In fact, it seemed like there were vehicles of every description. Cars, electric trolleys, bicycles (approximately 12 million in Shanghai alone, and all identical), donkeys, double-decker buses, and occasional rickshaws, and smelly old trucks that added even more pollution to the brown air we were breathing.

Their driving habits were amazing as well. In America when you make a U-turn, one is bounded by the curbs on the side of the road, but in Shanghai, there was so much traffic that the cabs were not only driving over the curbs, but right up the concrete staircases at the entrances to the department stores!

Something else that was unique to China . . . taking the elevator. First of all, . . . DON'T! The rules are different, different for citizens, different for tourists. What grabbed me was as we waited for the elevator and pressed the usual button, and . . . nothing. When it finally did arrive, the doors swung open, and there we stood, three Americans in search of almost anything. Someone inside said something short and quick in Chinese, and all the Chinese turned, stared, and exited the elevator. This was done because the Chinese people wanted to treat the American tourists as welcome guests in their country. At least that's what we were told. I, in turn, placed my hands in a prayerful position and swept my arm towards them in a welcoming way to encourage them to join us in the elevator. They would have none of that, although they remained all smiles. They just kept smiling and leaving the elevator each time we changed floors in the store.

On the second day of our trip, we were presented with a neat little note which told us we were going to take a day-long visit down the Li River in the province of Kweilin. It was a trip of about 50 miles and very picturesque. This winding river is bordered on both sides by strange looking saw-toothed mountains. It had been explained to us that we were going to have lunch onboard our stout sailing ship, which was actually a 100-foot ferryboat. I took a walk around the ship/boat, and noticed, with undue alarm, that there wasn't any restaurant on the boat. There was a small dining room, and I thought, "Awe shucks. It's going to be a bag lunch."

I needn't have worried because at about 11 a.m., four Chinese came up from below, dressed in white chef regalia, and started to lay out large platters on which were all kinds of luscious looking things. Oh yes, I almost forgot, they also set up a portable gas grill table, and that was when it started to get interesting.

The grill was set up in the stern of the boat in a roughly 10 foot square area. They worked very quickly, and before you knew it, a number of platters were heaped high with rice, chicken, shrimp, root vegetables, and some other things that were hard to identify.

Now keep in mind, this is a 100-foot vessel with about 100 people onboard. How do you feed 100 ravenous tourists from a small 10' by 10' area? Well, the only drawback to our delicious meal occurred when it came to sitting down; there were no chairs. But, would you believe it, they had everybody served, and the food was hot and delicious, although a couple of people nearly fell in the river when they lost their footing trying to spear a piece of something off their plates. Oh, I almost forgot, the cooks all assumed a squatting position as they cooked everything for the meal. It looked kind of crazy seeing four Chinese chefs squatting and cooking, but there was nothing crazy about the food they served.

A calamity almost occurred when one of the passengers started vomiting over the side of the boat, not once or twice, but by the fourth time, we lost count. That person was me. I was scared stiff as to what to do. There I was, sick as a dog on the Li River, in the middle of nowhere. My translator went to the captain's cabin and arranged for me to be taken off the ship, but I would have to wait until we had gone another 20 miles downriver.

Once off the boat, I climbed into some kind of staff car and was taken to an aid station, and boy, was I hurting. Then I was transferred by ambulance to the nearest local hospital. I remember it like it was yesterday. It was a cold and rainy day, and the hospital had stone floors – funny how I remember that – but it made it seem that much colder. I didn't like cold, wet and rainy places for a long time after that.

The doctor on duty was the saving grace for me. She listened to my tale of woe, asked me a few questions, and left the room. When she came back, she had a vial. Actually it was an old glass medicine bottle with a candle wax stopper. She gave me a shot in the arm and said to take the other dose remaining in the bottle sometime later in the afternoon. "Take it with some Coca Cola. They had just installed a Coke machine in the hospital lobby . . . lucky me.

I was then whisked off to the hotel and climbed into bed, clothes and all. At about 5 p.m., I was visited by my wife and a couple of traveling companions asking me if I was going to have some dinner.

"What? Are you CRAZY?" I quipped.

Then they asked me, "How do you feel, then?"

In a flash I suddenly realized that I was feeling pretty darn good. Kind of amazing, when you realize that six hours earlier, I thought I was going to die, and now here I was, talking and everything.

I had my wife call the hospital, with the help of an interpreter, to find out what kind of shot they gave me. Well, no wonder why I was feeling so good. The shot they gave me was pure laudanum, and laudanum is one step away from opium.

When they left for dinner, one of my friends commented that he thought he heard someone singing all afternoon, and I said, "Yeah, I guess that was me."

Then he asked, "Are you gonna take the rest of the prescription?"

I responded, "Are you serious? You go out and I'll stay right here. I *must* follow doctor's orders, you know!"

You might find it interesting that my wife stopped by the bank branch in our hotel to pick up some money to pay for whatever the charges would be for all the medical services I was rendered, due to my malady. I didn't know what the costs would be for the ambulance, the visit with the doctor and the laudanum, which I had already renamed "Joy juice."

Now let's see. I'll try to approximate the costs: Ambulance - $25. That's cheap for such a long trip; Consultation with the doctor - $20; and the medicine - $1,000. It was really more like $5.00, but it was worth at least $1,000 at the time (at least to me).

Now hold on to your seat. The bill actually totaled $3.87. They must be doing something right.

The next day, just before we left Kweilin, I penned a short note to the doctor to thank her for her expertise and her charming bedside manner.

A couple of weeks after I got back home, I received a short note from her thanking me for my thoughtfulness. It figures.

Just a couple of general comments about the food in China. It was, for the most part, delicious. Breakfast each day was the same. It was a serve-yourself buffet on large banquet tables laden with American and Chinese cuisine. I forget what they had on the American banquet table because I didn't eat anything American. It seemed to me kind of silly to fly 4,000 miles and eat scrambled eggs. I ate from the Chinese banquet table. Breakfast consisted of rice soup, which had generous pieces of chicken in it, and various vegetables served in big tureens. I didn't feel guilty stealing so many mushrooms - 1 love mushrooms - as there were so many vegetables in those giant tureens.

Speaking of mushrooms, I was told by my interpreter that we were going to get our fill of mushrooms on the plane ride from Kweilin to Canton. He gave us a heads-up on a special stopover for lunch in Changsha, the birthplace of Mao Tse Tung. On the ground, we exited the plane and walked across the tarmac, a pretty good distance to the airport restaurant. After eating a sumptuous lunch, I volunteered to go back and walk it again, so I could eat another fabulous meal. (They had the biggest mushrooms I'd ever seen in the rice soup). But don't take my word for how delicious the food is in China. The only way to really find out how good the food is . . . is to go there and taste it for yourself.

I visited China twice, once in the early 1980s, and then again in 1990. I can truthfully say that China changed a great deal in that one decade. My mind goes back to 1980 when I first visited and found the Chinese people as courteous as anywhere in the world. When I returned 10 years later, I was rather dismayed at the erosion of their kindly manners.

A good example of what China was like in the 80s is illustrated in the *Wallet Story*. It concerned a gentleman from Europe who had been visiting a local restaurant and, after having a few drinks, was alarmed to find that he had misplaced his wallet, somewhere in the restaurant he thought, or perhaps, it had been stolen.

"Not stolen, definitely not," said our guide, "We are not a den of thieves."

So, after giving the necessary description of the wallet and where he was staying to the tavern keeper, our guide paid for a taxi for the gentleman and he drove off to his hotel. We found out later, his hotel was only a few blocks away, so it only took a few minutes for him to arrive at his destination. Can you imagine being in a strange city, thousands of miles away from home, and misplacing your wallet? Can you imagine what a super feeling it was for him to walk into his hotel room and see his wallet right on top of his bed. How did they do that? Somehow, the missing wallet had been found and restored to the gentlemen in the time it took him to get back to his hotel room. Amazingly, Oh, I almost forgot, a phrase I heard many, many times in China to cover a bevy of situations, and our guide said it to us more than once, "In China we have a way of doing things."

I asked him how he managed to get the wallet back to the hotel before the gentleman got to his room, and he said it again. "In China we have a way of doing things," and he said it with a smile. It was the same smile I was to see many times while visiting that mysterious land.

It was a smile I looked for, and didn't see 10 years later, in 1990. It was amazing to me to see such a change in attitude over only 10 years. I don't mean that China had stopped smiling, but in so many cases that, "we treasure your visit with us," feeling was missing.

I am most often asked by folks who have never been to the Orient, "What's the most exciting, or just downright enjoyable, sight to see?"

Pat and Dave Maynard at the Wall.

You might think that the Great Wall would fill the bill, and while it's still an exciting thing to see, there is another fascinating piece of history that is a *must see,* and that is the 2,000 plus statues of The Terra Cotta Army, which is located in the northern province of Xian.

Just think. Over 2,000 soldiers made of terracotta (shown here as seen in the Travel China guide) created by the first Emperor of China to follow and safeguard him upon his passage into the netherworld. The average Chinese male is about 5'8", but through the Emperor's eyes, his soldiers were all at least six feet tall, each with his own amazingly different facial features.

After a while, I noticed something was missing. The terracotta soldiers were once adorned with weapons and armor, that, alas, had long ago been removed by warring tribes. Our Chinese guide assured me that another trip to his country was a must. After all, they were working on the dig that would eventually unearth another 2,000 warriors. "Amazing," said I, and I actually said to him, "And I know how you will do it, and I won't give your secret away, because many, many times when visiting your mysterious country I have heard over and over again, 'In China we have a way of doing things.'"

West of Red Square is the Great Hall of the People. Talk about grand . . . and amazing. The building is the site of the China National People's Congressional meetings. The hall had three parts; the Central Hall, the Great Auditorium and the Banqueting Hall. The floor of the Central Hall was paved with marble, and crystal chandeliers hung from the ceiling. The Hall will seat 10,000 people. The Banqueting Hall was just as impressive and served 5,000 people at a sitting. I guess when their government is in session they have very big parties.

Speaking of parties, I remember having a wonderful time at a party I threw the night before we were leaving for Hong Kong. We had a tremendous banquet and we were really amazed when, toward the end of the party, the hotel, brought out a record player, visited each table, and invited us to dance. Have you ever heard Chinese dance music? Pretty good, I guess. As for myself, I tried to dance, but I soon gave it up because the music of the samisen, which is a two string guitar, played solo, does not quite sound like Glenn Miller, but it was important that we at least tried.

Now comes the rest of the story. I haven't mentioned the presence of Miss Yung and Miss Woo, our tour guides. Miss Woo and Miss Yung were to stay with us every minute we were in China, and that made us happy. We were wonderfully informed and they always took the time to answer our many questions. They were so knowledgeable, and it was a joy to engage them in conversation. We were in good hands and I sometimes got the feeling that we wouldn't have had the carefree two weeks that we spent in China if Mr. Big had gone along with us. That being so, I made a decision, on my own, to reward these two young ladies, even though I had been warned (we all were) at least 120 times, not to give any kind of gratuity to our guides. I had, for some reason, brought a Kodak Brownie camera. As a matter of fact, I had two, and I thought to myself, what a lovely gift to give to each of them. We wrapped them up in toilet paper (Asking for wrapping paper in a store in China didn't make it). That night at the party we made a real hit with the cameras. What we should be hearing now is some ominous background music, because guess what? Mr. Big was in the house. That's right, Mr. Big, with his sharp but definite speech on the rules of giving. Very simple – Don't!

Next midday at the train station we were ready to board the train to Hong Kong. Miss Yung and Miss Woo were nowhere to be found. We had just one problem after I helped my tour group through the gate to the train. I was taken aside and prohibited from boarding with them. I was told the problem was that I had given a gift to the tour guides. I was being held back by the guards as my group was boarding the train. I shouted to them to let them know what was happening to me and why. One of my number certainly didn't help much. He walked up to the wrought iron fence and was taking photos of the Chinese guards holding me back from boarding the train. Just then, Mr. Big approached me and immediately told me to tell the gentlemen taking the photos to stop. He asked me, "Why did you give cameras to your guides?"

I responded, "They did a very good job," and I proceeded to describe to him what a wonderful job they had done for us. "It is just our way of saying, *Thank you.*" I told him I was very sorrowful, and felt badly that I would have to tell millions of Americans how poorly I was treated in China, and what a horrendous mistake it was to leave a gift for people who really deserved it. I told him, "I do a radio show which includes an audience of telephone callers from all across the United States. In addition," I told him, "I do a little television show as well, which has an audience of New Englanders that will undoubtedly have a lot to say regarding my predicament."

I could see that this had made an impression on him, and he had a conversation with the two suits who had accompanied him to the train station. There was a lot of nodding and posturing, and - get this - all the while this was going on, I'm standing there pleading to Mr. Big and his two cohorts and one Chinese soldier holding a rifle, to let me board the train. Meanwhile on the other side of the wrought iron fence, 40 *very* upset Americans, one of whom was now leading some kind of chant shouting how many minutes were remaining until the train departed. Just what I wanted to hear.

Then, all of a sudden, Mr. Big came over to me and, with a wave of his hand, I could tell he was going to let me board the train. He said, "I hope you will visit us again."

I said, "I will."

He said, "I hope to hear your radio show one day, and by the way, (I don't know what made him say this) have you ever heard of William Shakespeare?"

I said, "I beg your pardon?" I had taken a course in Shakespeare in college and was required to memorize 67 passages from Hamlet.

He said, "Never mind. Next time perhaps."

I don't know to this day why he asked me that, but I thought about it and it almost made me snicker thinking maybe he was trying to offer a bit of class. Try this: "Oh that this too, too solid flesh would melt and thaw itself into a dew." *Thank you Hamlet.*

Chapter 7

HUMOR

I wanted to include some short humorous stories and one-liners I used on my radio show over the years. For some of you, these will ring familiar, for the rest, just sit back and enjoy. They will give you the flavor of my show, regardless of the time slot I was in at any particular time. By the way, after we finished this chapter, I fully expected the next time I called Suzan (and I was surprised she answered), I was sure that she would be long gone to Chicago doing standup.

Strudel Anyone?

Bud Wiegele says old man Sam was nearing the end of a long life, and as he rested, he decided it was time to call his children to his side. They stood around his bed, waiting for him to speak.

"Children, your mother and I have been married for more than 50 years," Sam said, "but you should know she made my life miserable. She was a real bad apple. It was a terrible life I had."

One of the sons was shocked at hearing this news and wanted to know why he stayed married to her if everything was as bad as he insisted.

"Because she could bake and cook like an angel," Sam said. "Even now, I can smell a strudel baking. Sarah, be a good girl and go get you dying father a piece of strudel."

Sam closed his eyes and waited for Sarah's return. When he heard her come into the room, he opened his eyes.

"Sarah, where's the strudel? Sam said.

"Mom says you can't have any."

"Why not?"

"She says it's for the funeral tomorrow."

-author Alex Thien of the Milwaukee Sentinel, 9/11/1985

Will Rogers's Kind of Politics

More than 50 years after his death, some of Will Rogers' remarks remain fresh.

On foreign relations: "Now if there is one thing that we do worse than any other nation, it is trying to manage somebody else's affairs."

On elections: "A flock of Democrats will replace a mess of Republicans. It won't mean a thing. They will go in like all the rest of 'em. Go in on promises and come out on alibis."

On old fashioned colleges: "They even had reading, writing and 'rithmetic, instead of football. Up to then, boys had gone there for their heads and not their shoulders."

On the Soviet Union: "They are studying some devilment to pull on the rest of the world. A Russian just loves misery and he wants to get as many in on it as he can."

On hunger: "The Lord so constituted everybody that no matter what color you are, you require about the same amount of nourishment."

From an article in The Omaha World- Herald, 9/5/85

Old Age is Hell - A poem

The body gets stiff, you get cramps in your legs,
Corns on your feet, as big as hens' eggs.
Gas on your stomach, elimination is poor
Take Ex-Lax at night and then you're not sure.

You soak in the tub or your body will smell,
It's like I said folks, OLD AGE IS HELL.
Your teeth start decaying, your eyesight is poor,
Hair falling out, all over the floor.
Sex life is short. It's a thing of the past,
Don't kid yourself friend, even that don't last.
Can't go to parties, don't dance anymore,
Just to put things mildly, you're a hell of a bore.
Liquor is out, can't take a chance,
Your bladder is weak, might pee in your pants.
Nothing to plan for, nothing to expect,
(Just the mailman with your Social Security Check.)

Now be sure your affairs are in order, and your will is made right,
Or on the way to the graveyard, there will be a hell of a fight.
You feel pretty good, you look fairly well,
Thank God you're alive, OLD AGE IS HELL!

Author Unknown

Sex Survey

I was as shocked as you to read last week that a survey of 236 married couples indicated more women (26%) enjoyed sex than enjoyed "sewing for leisure" (25%).

Needless to say, a far greater number (37%) preferred reading to either activity, although, as one woman I know put it succinctly, "It depends on the book."

The survey, as reported by two sociologists in *The Journal of Sexual Research,* also showed that more men (45%) claimed in their macho fashion that they liked sex better than anything, even watching television.

But why sex should edge out sewing among women is difficult to comprehend. Sewing, after all, is a calm, restful, highly productive pursuit and afterward, if you haven't made a mistake, you have something to show for it. Sex is just the opposite.

Henny Youngman

Henny Youngman checks in with the story of a young man who applied for a job at an ad agency. He was told, "Your resume is full of distortions, half-truths and bald faced lies. Welcome aboard."
Irv Kupcinet from the Chicago Sun Times, 3/5/84

Dave's Do's and Don'ts

Bloopers

Don't do what a National Radio announcer did about 25 years ago:
At 4:55 p.m., we prepared to switch the feed to Churchill Downs where the Kentucky Derby is held. I kept my eyes on the clock to switch over to the Kentucky Derby at 5 p.m. on the straight up. It was then, as I started to get up from my chair to leave, that the national radio made this announcement:

"Hello America, and welcome to the sixth running of the Canturky Dubby."

Remember, this broadcast was nationwide and I started laughing so hard, I couldn't get all the way up out of my seat. I had to sit back down until I could finally stop laughing.

Paraphrasing an article by Rep. Hinshaw in the Congressional Record

"In the beginning, God created the heaven and earth. Quickly he was faced with a class-action suit for failure to file an Environmental Impact Statement. He was granted a temporary permit for the heavenly part of the project, but was stymied with a Cease and Desist Order for the earthly part.
Appearing at the hearing, God was asked why he began the Earthly Project in the first place. He replied that he just liked to be creative.
Then God said, "Let there be light" and immediately the officials demanded to know how the light would be made. Would there be strip mining? What about thermal pollution? God explained that light would come from a huge ball of fire.

God was granted provisional permission to make light, assuming that no smoke would result from the ball of fire, and that he would obtain a building permit and, to conserve energy, would have the light out half the time.

God agreed and said he would call the light, "Day," and the darkness, "Night."

Officials replied that they weren't interested in semantics.

God said, "Let the earth bring forth green herb and such as may seed."

The E.P.A. agreed so long as native seed was used.

Then God said, "Let the waters bring forth creeping creatures having life and the fowl that may fly over the earth."

Officials pointed out that this would require approval of the Fish and Game Commission, with the Heavenly Wildlife Federation and The Audubongelic Society.

So everything was okay until God said he wanted to complete the project in six days. Officials said it would take at least one hundred eighty days to review the application and the impact statement. After that there would be public hearings. Then there would be ten to twelve months before . . .

God said, "To H--- with it!"

One liners, Etc.

1. "I like being confused. It sharpens my hearing." -Jimmy Durante

2. The telephone and electric bill should be printed on paper towels. That way when you get your bill, you can start crying immediately. -*Author Unknown*

3. Sign in an Art Gallery: "We hung this picture because we couldn't find the Artist." -*Author Unknown*

4. Don't move. I want to forget you, just the way you are. -*Author Unknown*

5. Richard Simmons was run out of town by the Welcome Wagon. -*Author Unknown*

6. Things are getting better, because things are getting worse slower. -*Author Unknown*

7. The prescription instructions said, "Take one pill as often as you can afford it." -*Author Unknown*

8. Female driver to passenger: "Look out the window and see if we're close enough to the curb." Response: "We're within walking distance." *-Author Unknown*

9. Bumper Sticker: "Start a movement, drink prune juice." *-Author Unknown*

10. The word, "deficit," is in the news these days. Ty Kuhn defines it this way: "It's what you got when you haven't got as much as you had when you had nothing." *-Rod O'Donnell, Nashville Banner, 1983*

11. The secret of success is this: There is no secret of success. *-Elbert Hubbard recalled*

12. Our gauge of success is not whether you have a tough problem to handle, but whether it is the same problem you had last year. *-General Motors (quoted by Gene Brown, Danbury Connecticut News-Times)*

13. "It's vacation season again and there is one essential question to answer before you go to a foreign land: Can you drink the water when you get there?" "If you want to look like them, drink the water, -W.C. Fields

14. A lot of American tourists believe they have to avoid water entirely. So they end up using the W.C. Fields method. Fields refused to drink water, he said, because fish made love in it. So he drank only booze instead.

"Drink whisky and nothing else," a friend advised me before I left for my first trip to the Mideast. "Never have drinks with ice cubes. Never brush your teeth with anything but Scotch. And keep your mouth shut in the shower. A lot of people forget that."

"What about thunderstorms," I asked. "Is it okay to keep your mouth open when it rains?"

He thought for a moment, and then responded, "Not if the clouds are local."

I told my friend there was a problem with his all-booze method. "If you drink all day, you tend to miss things."

"Like what?" he demanded. "I spent two weeks in Egypt drinking nothing but whisky and I didn't miss a thing."

"So what did you think of the pyramids," I asked.

"Pyramids?" he said. "Egypt has pyramids?"

-Roger Simon, Milwaukee Sentinel, 1983

15. DRACULA, THE ORIGINAL IRS TRAINING FILM. *-Author Unknown*

16. Why do they call it rush hour when no one's moving? – *Author Unknown*

17. Lou Holtz, the University of Minnesota football coach, told Life Magazine: "I don't let my players do those crazy dances in the end zone. I want them to act like they've been there before." *–Irv Kupcinet, Chicago Sun-Times, 1984*

18. Astonishing the number of live-together couples who are getting married in the wake of the Lee Marvin trial. The men apparently figure that community property is a better bet in the long run than a lawsuit. *–Herb Caen, San Francisco Chronicle, 1979*

19. Praise is the easiest way to get anybody's attention. *–Gene Brown, Danbury, Conn. News Times, 1979*

20. English isn't such a hard language to learn. It's all built around one simple expression: "Ya' know?" *–Cincinnati Enquirer, 1979*

21. A person who can speak many languages is not as valuable as a person who can listen well in one. *–Frank Tyger, Wall Street Journal, 1979*

22. "The fuel shortage is worse than many of us think," said J.W. Irvin of the Metro Police Department. "The other night I got a call from a fellow who reported he had been mugged for the fluid in his cigarette lighter!" *–Red O'Donnell, Nashville Banner, 1979*

23. If you believe in reincarnation, you positively know that in a previous life, Imelda Marcos was a centipede. *-Irv Kupcinet, Chicago Sun-Times, 1986*

24. A fellow who works on the AIDS hot line got a call from a nervous chap who wondered if it's possible to get AIDS from killer bees. "Only if you have sex with the queen," replied the quick thinker. *-Herb Caen, San Francisco Chronicle, 1985*

25. You are middle-aged when you hear two conflicting voices. One asks, "Why not?" The other, "Why bother?" *-Elaine Reetz, Waushara, WI, Argus, 1985*

26. Tonight on TV: Cable will show their new Game Show, "Gay Newlyweds." *-Author Unknown*

27. My Cardiologist has a heart-shaped pool. My Urologist has a kidney-shaped pool. My Proctologist has a little Jacuzzi. *-Author Unknown*

28. Why worry about Russia? Who would be dumb enough to bomb Washington and end all the confusion? *-Author Unknown*

29. Remember, no matter how much cosmetic surgery you have done, you'll still have ugly babies. *-Author Unknown*

30. The 88 percent turnout for the Chicago election was a surprise. Some politicians had expected 110 percent of the voters to cast ballots. *-Wendell Trogdon, The Indianapolis News, 1983*

31. It's our one man's opinion: Our young people should know there still is a good reason for getting married. It's the best way to get acquainted. *-Author Unknown*

32. Dustin Hoffman's movie, "Tootsie," is being heralded through the nation as a great comedy, except in San Francisco. There they think it's a documentary. *-Author Unknown*

33. If you look at a gorilla in the zoo long enough, he'll remind you of somebody you know. *-Irv Kupcinet, Chicago Sun-Times, 1985*

34. A Frenchman, a Japanese and an American face a firing squad. Offered a last wish, the Frenchman asks to hear the Marseillaise. The Japanese asks to give one more lecture on Japanese management. The American asks to be shot first. "I can't stand one more lecture on Japanese management," he said. *-Herm Albright, The Perry Township Weekly, Ind.,1983*

35. Automobile racing is okay, but they'd liven things up some if they'd put a few Sunday drivers, oil trucks and jalopies pulling boat trailers on the racetracks, so that the drivers would have to face the same dangers that all the rest of us do. *-Ashley Cooper, Charleston New Courier, SC, 1979*

36. "When you're broke, nobody gives you a bean. Soon as you get rich, they won't let you pay." *–John Wayne*

37. A while ago, while driving in central Wisconsin, we caught up to an Amish carriage with an owner who obviously had a sense of humor. Attached to the back of the carriage was a hand-lettered sign that said, "Energy efficient vehicle. Runs on oats and grass. Caution: Do not step on exhaust." *-Sandy Cooley, New Holstein Reporter, WI, 1987*

38. Q: Why does the Legislature meet in January and February? A: Because the weather usually is too bad to play golf. *-Wendell Trogdon, The Indianapolis News, 1986*

39. Secretary of State George Schultz, according to the New York Times, told the House Foreign Affairs Committee that he would like to use a joke to illustrate the administration's problem with restarting the Middle East peace talks. The story went like this: "Why did the Frenchman kiss the lady's hand? The answer," Mr. Schultz said, was that, "You have to start somewhere."

40. A former basketball coach says that he went through some lean years with a few of his teams. "I was at one school and we just couldn't seem to win at all," he said. "I came home once after the team had taken a awful shellacking and my kid – he was about 6 years old at the time – said to me, 'You ain't a very good coach, are you Daddy?' The only thing I could think to say to him was "Don't say *ain't*." -*Author Unknown*

41. As you grow old, your beauty (if any) fades, your skin sags, your features droop, your strength diminishes, your agility ends, your sense of smell and hearing decreases, your hair and teeth fall out, your joints ache . . . and that's only if you have perfect health.-*Ashley Cooper, Charleston News and Courier, SC, 1980*

42. Steve Jarrell sends these excerpts from "Mother Murphy's Law and Other Perils of Parenthood."

First law of parenthood: Nobody really wants your job, but everybody thinks they can do it better.

Limits of endurance: You don't know what the limits of your endurance are until you've had children. From infancy on, your children will discover those limits and push you beyond them.

The grandparents' vindication: You can never appreciate your parents' hard work and sacrifice until you have children of your own. That's why your parents are so happy when you have children.

The transportation tangle: The baby in the carriage will want to climb out. The baby in the backpack will want to walk. The child on foot will want to be carried. The child on the trike will want to ride a two-wheeler. The teenager on the 10-speed will want your car. The teenager with your car will want a sports car.

The floor fascination factor: If it's on your floor, it will wind up in your baby's mouth. If it's in your baby's mouth, it will wind up on your floor.

The sanitary solution: When your first baby drops her pacifier, you sterilize it and wash the baby. When your second baby drops his pacifier, you pick it up off the floor, wipe it off on your shirt and pop it back into his mouth. When your third baby drops her pacifier, you let the dog fetch it for her.

The sharing statute: The toy your toddler ignored for months will suddenly become his favorite toy the minute another child reaches for it.

The dental dilemma: The best time to schedule dental appointments for your teenagers is during their toughest class. Otherwise they won't go.

The drink dilemma: It is impossible to pour drinks for two pre-schoolers perfectly equally. No snack time is complete without the inevitable question, "How come he got more than me?" -*Ashley Cooper, Charleston News and Courier, SC, 1987*

43. Definition of a pedestrian: A guy who expected his son to fill the gas tank. -*Wayne Mackey, Oklahoma City Times, 7/26/1983*

44. Candidate Bentsen was told, "When you become Vice President, you're required to notify the IRS, the Secret Service and the Bureau Of Missing Persons." -*Author Unknown*

45. The only way to combat criminals is . . . stop voting for them. -*Alexander The Weenie, Chicago, Ill.*

46. There's no sure formula of success in this business. A friend of mine never hit it big, even though he's the image of Phyllis Diller. -*Alexander The Weenie, Chicago, Ill.*

47. I know some folks who, if there were a nip in the air . . . would drink it. -*Lou Erickson, Atlanta Journal, 12/23/72*

48. A bachelor is a man who has not yet had all of his faults

pointed out to him. -*Hugh Allen, Knoxville News Sentinel, 7/15/72*

What NOT to do in a job interview

Some things change and some things stay the same:

In a few weeks, another batch of graduates will get chewed up job-hunting because their schools left them greener than a gourd about interviewing gamesmanship. I have included this section to help advise all those newbie's looking for employment, and also give them a good laugh while doing so. Good luck, and don't make these mistakes.

Honesty isn't so much the issue as how much to show of the "real you." This world may not be ready for the real you. A job interview is no time to do your Boy George imitation. Employment expert, Robert Half, hired Cincinnati-based Burke Marketing Research to survey personnel directors and top executives from

100 of America's largest corporations on "the most unusual thing a candidate ever did in an interview." Here are some responses:

-While I was on a long phone call, candidate casually put a box of Kentucky Fried Chicken on my desk and started eating.

-Brought his mother into the room for the interview.

-Had a little pinball game. He challenged me to a game.

-He wouldn't get out of the chair until I would hire him, I had to call the police.

-When I asked about his hobbies, he stood up and started tap dancing around my office (Must have been one of my Community Auditions winners).

-Pulled out a Polaroid camera and snapped a flash picture of me. Said he collected photos of everyone who interviewed him.

-Told me if I didn't hire her, she'd have her grandmother put a curse on me.

-When I refused to make a job offer, he tried to hit me.

From Tony Lang, The Cincinnati Enquirer, May 2, 1985

Chapter 8

Star Spotter

What follows in the next couple of paragraphs is living proof that what I've been saying all along is true. I can spot a star faster than anybody else. How do you sharpen your ability to do this? It's simple. Keep your eyes open and don't be overbearing.

I haven't spotted any stars for about ten years. Take it easy. I was just kidding. Whenever I go to New York for any reason, I always try to have at least one meal, preferably dinner, at a steak house on First Avenue named Billy's. It's also a watering hole and a super place to have a three martini lunch, if you can find a buddy to drink with. It's also a perfect location to become a Dave Maynard Star Spotter.

One success happened when I spotted a very handsome gentlemen of about 40 at Billy's. He was a motion picture star, a super singer and, as I found out a little bit later, a great conversationalist and joke teller. When I approached him, something told me that this man was going to show a friendly spirit. I certainly picked a winner because he was as friendly as could be. He ordered me a drink and I took it and drank it. Of course I ordered him one and we spent the next three to four hours having a great time. By now I bet you're getting a little impatient as to who I spent such a great afternoon with: Identification coming up. Once again my Star Spotter instinct had stuck again. His name was Gordon MacRae.

It saddened me no end, to see his obituary a few years later in the New York Times and on about ten television channels. He was a star, no doubt about that, so I ordered a drink for him even though he was buried in Nebraska, and I was home in Boston.

Gordon MacRae fell into the category of a very gifted and talented human being. He was tall, dark, and handsome. As for his singing voice, honest to God, as I sat in that bar in NYC, I can remember his bursting into the song, *I Surrender Dear,* and that's a 50-year old memory, no flats or sharps, and to top it off, that dazzling smile.

There was something else that Gordon MacRae had, and that was a great sense of humor, and he really proved it that day. It was 1 p.m., lunch time, and we were, as I said, at Billy's. We had just started our second martini when into this lovely cafe strode a statuesque blonde, and boy, she was some looker.

There we were at the bar, two of us ogling that very impressive lady. "I bet you $10 you can't get that lady to say hello to you," said Gordon.

"I'll bet you that same 10 bucks that says I can. You're Gordon MacRae, star of stage, screen and radio, and I'm just a schmuck from Boston, but I'm still going to win this bet."

He said, "You're On."

I slipped off my seat at the bar and confidently made my way to the end of the bar where she was seated. I said, "How do you do, my name is Dave Maynard. I'm from Boston, and if you can spare me 60 seconds, I'll tell you why I'm standing here." I told her about the $10 bet and promised she wouldn't have to move, as I would bring my antagonist to her.

She said, "Okay."

I thought, *It's in the bag.* I shall never forget introducing Gordon MacRae to his statuesque . . . beautiful . . . blonde . . . wife, Sheila. Although I might have been $10 richer, sometimes one wins the battle, but loses the war.

I'm sure it's happened to you. I'm doubly sure it's happened to me and I'll tell you why right away. There are certain people you think you have figured out. You just *know* what kind of people they are, even though you have never met them. I'm lucky. I got a chance to meet many celebrities and, I must admit, when I figured some of them wrong, it was very disconcerting. I'll give you an example. The person I have in mind was in every sense a movie star – tall, fair and handsome. Very outgoing. You know, the type of guy who you could have a conversation with and, just as soon it ended, forget it ever happened. The type of person who you might ask, "How are you?" and hope the answer will take a long time, rather than one word.

Now a little more about his looks. I already told you he was a knockout, and here's a big hint to our star puzzle. It has been said more than once, that he had the most beautiful eyes in moviedom. *This*, I had to see for myself. He was coming to the WBZ-TV studio, and of course, as soon as I heard this I started making plans on how I could affect a meeting between me, Gaga-Dave, and Academy Award winning actor, director, entrepreneur, Mr. Paul Newman.

Paul was born in January of 1925 and passed away in September, 2008, but his legacy still lives on. He was a founder of *Newman's Own* brand food products. you know, salad dressing, popcorn etc., and donated all the profits of the company to charity, which by the end of 2011 exceeded over $300 million in donations.

The big day came and I had my producer, Jack King, all set. I had to make sure that my secret passage from Studio A at WBZ-TV and Studio 1A on the radio side of the building was free of any obstacles, human beings included. Also, that my MacArthur Park record, 7 minutes, 30 seconds long, was ready to be played when I made my mad dash to the television side of the building.

There he was, standing right in the middle of the studio, and up I walked, bold as brass. Our noses almost touching, eyeball to eyeball, and do you know what I said to him? "Holy Jesus, It's True!"

And he said, "Ain't that a bitch!"

The year was 1965 and well, here I was once again, at one of my most favorite steakhouses in New York. I'm naturally referring to Billy's on First Avenue on the East side. We entered, some friends and I, around 4:30 p.m., and ordered a drink. We moved to one of the tables to order our second drink and dinner, and somehow the waiter brought us, for some ungodly reason, a third round of martinis.

Trouble! Everybody knows that if martini number three should pass your lips before 6:30 p.m., it's asking for DEEP TROUBLE.

We ordered our food which was easy enough to do. The first course was brought to the table, and I had a little trouble recognizing what it was, plated before me. One of us had ordered clam chowder, another (by the way there were three of us) ordered chili, and I asked for some pea soup, and you know what – they all looked the same! We solved this small dilemma by passing around the dishes. Of course, as I said, they were all the same, so it really didn't matter. We each took two spoonfuls and passed it around for the next person to try. It was like we were playing musical appetizers.

I can truthfully say, to this day, I cannot remember the three entrées, so let's just say steak. After all, it was a steakhouse.

And then it happened. Right in the middle of our steak, a loud, angry voice was heard. I have pretty good hearing, but you didn't need it to hear this woman. When that someone yells "Shit!" you have no trouble hearing her at all. There was a loud, noisy group with her of about five people. Believe me it wasn't a strain to hear them when those loudmouths were seated just two tables away from ours.

I remember, it hit me like a ton of bricks – star-spotter Dave had struck again. The name of this game was the belting mezzo-soprano with perfect pitch, Ethel Merman, and I contented myself to just sit there and stare at her . . . ogling. It wasn't a very nice thing to do but, what the hell. It *was* Ethel Merman, the undisputed star of the musical stage and screen, noted for her powerful voice and signature song, *There's No Business Like Show Business,* and besides, I was a fan and felt I was due.

That didn't last long. She looked up and saw my fond gaze and said in her strident voice, "What the f**k are *you* looking at!"

I said, "Right now, not a Hell of a lot."

Then, with a harrumph, she got up from the table, (I thought she was going to slug me) and disappeared.

No wonder Ernest Borgnine, star of the TV sitcom, *McHale's Navy* from 1962 thru 1967, could only stand to be married to her for 32 days before filing for a divorce.

Chapter 9

Dave's Health Tips

I wanted to share with you some intriguing and useful references to some health tips I've come across in my many years on radio and television. If you choose to try them, I'm sure they will work for some of you, but, alas, I can't guarantee they will work for everyone. I do know they have worked for many of my listeners, so keep an open mind and give them a try. After all, what have you got to lose?

Wine - The New Panacea

Stomach griping? Try a glass or two of a dry white wine such as Gaillac with meals.

Gripped by the grippe? Try the grape and heat a bottle of *Cotes du Rhone* in a double boiler, add cinnamon and sugar and lemon rind, drink a total of half a bottle three or four times a day.

Old rocking chair got you? Red Burgundy and Champagne, taken on alternate days are good for old age.

Gout? Well there's no proof that eating and drinking cause it, so have two glasses of *Sancerre, Pouilly*, or a *Rose de Provence* with meals.

And remember as you uncork the prescribed tipple, you *are* following doctor's orders. Americans are just catching onto the therapeutic properties of wine, but French physicians have long been using it to heal themselves. No profession includes a heartier group of trenchermen. French medical directories list membership in as many societies devoted to the table as to healing, and medical reviews often include recipes for rich and complicated dishes.

Dr. E.A. Maury of the *Faculte de Medecine* in Paris has done the sensible thing and written a book called, *Soignes-Vour par le Vin* (Treat Yourself with Wine), published by the *Editions de Jour* in Paris and giving vinous remedies for seventy-one ailments.

Citing medical authorities; from Dr. Nussbaum, who studies the low incidence of coronary disease in wine-drinking countries; to Professor Crawford of London, who demonstrated the dread connection between tap water and heart trouble; Dr. Maury states definitively that a wine of good quality, taken in reasonable amounts, will never produce ill effects on the organs. Wine, he says, quoting Louis Pasteur, is the best and healthiest of all beverages.

Even though he was a resident of the Royal Homeopathic Hospital of London and has had two of his works, *A Concise Guide to Homeopathy*, and *Drainage in Homeopathy*, translated into English, Dr. Maury is plainly against distilled liquors, which eliminates not only the wee dram of whiskey so often recommended for circulatory ailments in the United States, but also practical elixirs made by Marist Brothers in a Rhone village that had been recommended for both internal and external use; rubbed on the skin, it helps sprains or insect bites, when swallowed it dissipates chills and stomach ache.

Dr. Maury analyzes wines from their chemical content and also finds them full of vitamins.

"Is it not better," he asks, "to absorb your natural vitamins in a good glass of wine than to take them in pills?"

Keep talking doc.

Specific remedies suggested by Dr. Maury include:

For allergies: half a glass of Medoc at meals for its rich potassium content;

For anemia: two glasses of *Cotes de Graves* with meals for its rich iron content;

For sore throat: warmed up Medoc or *Beaujolais* because they soothe, decongest, and kill bacteria;

For bronchitis: warmed-up Bordeaux or Burgundy because of their phosphorous content;

For constipation: white wines from Anjou or Vouvray to activate the intestines;

For fever: a bottle of champagne a day; and

For obesity: a daily bottle of *Rose de Provence*, half with each meal.

Dr. Maury does not feel that a good wine in moderate doses could ever cause cirrhosis, but he does seem to go along with the old French custom in considering Bordeaux the most therapeutic of wines, prescribing it for 24 ailments ranging from loss of appetite to typhoid fever!

Bordeaux is much in demand these days as a cure for fatigue, according to both the veteran wine merchant, Lucien Legrand and Steven Spurrier, the English Proprietor of the *Caves de la Madeleine*.

"People are always coming in for something to energize themselves, a pick-me-up" says Mr. Spurrier. "Bordeaux is the only wine that energizes because of its balance between vegetable and alcoholic content. Bordeaux is also supposed to be slightly more digestible because it is slightly higher in tannins, which tea also provides."

Dr. Maury does not limit himself to Bordeaux in treating ailments of the mind rather than the body. While he recommends a red Medoc (one or two glasses before and during meals) for a nervous breakdown, and the side effects of menopause, he thinks neurasthenia is best handled by a half bottle daily of *Blanquette de Limoux*, taken between meals.

Wine may be a mocker, but it is not a killer, insists Dr. Maury in his rather florid style. "The juice of the wine," he writes, "is constantly condemned; it is cited as the source of an infinity of evils, starting with alcoholism and ending with increased criminality and road accidents. And yet, the Lord knows that never in the history of humanity have so much water and fruit juice been consumed."

In conclusion, name your poison, or stick with the good doctor and raise your glass to drink to his, and your own, very good health: *A votre sante*, as they've been saying here for years!

-Taken from an article that appeared in Vogue Magazine,
November, 1977

The Cabbage Soup Diet

Back in 1996, I let people know about this new diet craze. After talking about this on the radio for a couple of days, I received over 50,000 requests for the diet both by phone and by mail. I thought you might like to see what it was all about.

The soup recipe calls for a whole head of cabbage plus celery, green onions, green beans, green peppers and crushed tomatoes.

Beside the soup, certain other foods can also be eaten each day, but in limited quantities -- fruit one day; all vegetables and a buttered baked potato the next; fruit and vegetables on the third day; eight bananas and skim milk the next day; beef and tomatoes the next two days; and brown rice and vegetables on the seventh day.

Dr. Tom Cooper, an Atlanta-based weight loss expert, says, "The Cabbage Soup Diet can take away that empty feeling when the munchy monster comes after you."

Some copies of the diet claim it is from the Sacred Heart Medical Center in Spokane, Washington. But Elaine Reid, director of food and nutrition at the center, denies rumors that the crash diet was created for their overweight heart patients. She adds that she even received a call from a representative of Arnold Schwarzenegger when the actor was chairman of the President's Council on Physical Fitness and Sports, who wondered if the actor should endorse it.

Reid agrees with other doctors and nutritionists who warn that the diet plan isn't nutritionally balanced and "could be harmful to heart patients because of the enormous 20 ounce limit of beef and the high-sodium content in the onion soup mix."

But many people who need to lose weight fast claim it's the diet fad that won't die. The cabbage brew, water and vegetables are pure and healthy and many dieters say that they're willing to sacrifice a week on the diet to drop 10 to 17 pounds without starving or working out.

Finally, as with any diet, it's best to consult your doctor before you begin.

Since it was so overwhelmingly popular and drew so much interest on the radio, I'm repeating the recipe here, but you don't get any guarantees from me.

Cabbage Soup Recipe

½ to whole head cabbage
One 28 oz. can crushed or diced tomatoes
6 onions
1 package Lipton Onion Soup Mix
2 green bell peppers
1 bunch of scallions
1 bunch of celery
6 carrots (optional)
16 oz. green beans (optional)
1 to 2 cubes of beef or chicken bouillon, or 1 can V-8 or tomato juice and ½ cup balsamic vinegar (both optional)
Herbs to taste
Black pepper to taste

Chop vegetables, combine all ingredients in a stockpot, and add enough water to cover. Boil 10 minutes. Reduce to a simmer and continue cooking until vegetables are tender. Makes about six quarts. Eat as much as you want whenever you want, at any time of the day.

Nutritional information per cup (with the minimum additions: 34 calories; 1 gram protein; 8 grams carbohydrate; trace fat; 64 mg. sodium.

This is the 7 day diet plan. All versions of it say to eat as much soup as you want throughout the week. Add the following foods:

Day 1: All fruits except bananas. Cantaloupe and watermelon are lower in calories than most fruit. Eat only our soup, fruit and unsweetened tea, cranberry juice or water.

Day 2: Eat all the fresh vegetables you want, raw or cooked, along with your soup (but no fruit). Stick to leafy green vegetables and stay away from dried beans, peas and corn. You may also have a large baked potato with butter on your vegetable day.

Day 3: Fruits and vegetables. No potatoes or bananas.

Day 4: Along with your soup, eat as many as eight bananas and drink as many glasses of skim milk as you can.

Day 5: Beef, chicken (without skin) or fish. You can eat 10 to 20 ounces of beef, chicken or fish and as many as six fresh tomatoes. Drink at least six to eight glasses of water. Be sure to eat the soup at least once.

Day 6: Eat beef, chicken (without skin) or fish to your heart's content with leafy greens, but no baked potato. As on Day 5, be sure to drink water and eat soup.

Day 7: Dig into as much brown rice, vegetables and unsweetened fruit juice as you want. Have at least one serving of soup. At the end of the seventh day, if you haven't cheated, you'll have lost 10 to 17 pounds. If you have lost more than 15 pounds, stay off the diet for at least two days.

This diet does not allow alcoholic drinks at any time. Go off the diet at least 24 hours before any intake of alcohol. Although you can drink black coffee, you may find you won't need caffeine after the third day.

No substitutions. That means no bread and no carbonated beverages, not even diet soda.

Drink water, unsweetened tea, black coffee, unsweetened fruit juice, cranberry juice and skim milk (on the day allowed). No fried foods. All meats must be broiled or baked.

- This diet from an Article in Star Magazine, April 9, 1996

A word to the wise: If your doctor has said to avoid certain foods for any reason, follow your doctor's instructions.

Why Beer is Better than Women

1. You don't have to wine and dine a beer.
2. Your beer will always wait patiently for you in the car while you play football.
3. Beer hangovers go away.
4. A beer doesn't get jealous when you grab another beer.
5. Beer and poker always go together.
6. When you go to a bar you always know you can pick up a beer.
7. Beer never has a headache.
8. After you've had a beer, the bottle is still worth 10 cents.
9. A beer won't get upset if you come home and have another beer on your breath.
10. You can have more than one beer in a night, and not feel guilty.
11. You can share a beer with your friends.
12. Beer doesn't demand equality.
13. You can have a beer in public.

14. A frigid beer is a good beer.
15. If you change beers, you don't have to pay alimony.

For All That Ails You

I don't know why . . . wait a minute . . . I do remember why and I remember very well when somebody called in the middle of the night, because I had said on the air that I had a bad back. I asked, no, I begged, whether or not there was anyone listening who had a remedy for this aching malady, which did not allow me to lie down, stand up, walk, run or even sit without really excruciating pain – a pain so severe which forced me to hire a young, strong physical therapist who would carry me to the bathroom. A little embarrassing, but when you consider the alternative (for example, not making it to the bathroom on time), he was my savior.

One night in response to my cry for help with my back pain someone called and asked if I had ever heard of DMSO or Dimethylsulfoxide.

I answered, "No."

"Well," he said, "I bet you'll get a lot of calls after I hang up telling you of the magical powers of this horse liniment," and did we ever.

Off and on for the next three months or so, I would do at least an hour or two on the efficacy of DMSO on my radio program.

I'll give you a few examples of what kind of experiences people had when they used DMSO as a pain reliever.

One caller shared that his Dad had terrible arthritis pain in his entire body. He went to a chiropractor and was hopeful for some pain relief. Believe it or not, this is what his son told us on the air. The chiropractor recommended DMSO. "However," he warned, "this liniment is not approved by the FDA for people, only horses."

Now get this. I don't know who gave him the idea of application, but he first applied the ointment on his shoulder area and, in a couple of days, some of the pain in his shoulder had left. Next, he applied the DMSO to his hip; same application, same result . . . relief! Next he applied it to his knees; same result. Last he applied the liniment to his ankle and toes, and the pain went out through the bottom of his feet.

There will be many people, upon hearing this, who will say to themselves . . . Ah . . . Bologna! After all, people don't use horse liniment. Well, think again. Here is another story.

One fellow called and he had another short, but sweet story to tell. He worked in a local stable in rural Massachusetts, and he noticed after treating the horses with DMSO, that his hands which had been terribly afflicted by arthritis, became pretty much pain-free, along with a reduction in the swelling.

Another caller told me that he had finally convinced his father to use the medication, because his father had terrible problems driving a car because of acute pain in his hands and forearms. He lived in Miami, and I tell you this because one month later, I received a letter from the son who was extremely happy. He reported to me that not only had his father's arthritic pain come under control, but at 75-years-old, he drove from Miami to Boston . . . solo.

You can buy DMSO almost anywhere now, but at the time finding DMSO solvent was extremely difficult. In fact we had to go to an animal husbandry co-op to purchase it back then. Remember to carefully follow the instructions.

The following is the information I have to share with you about DMSO: DMSO SOLVENT 99.7% PURE Pharmaceutical Grade.

General Information: In the early 1950s Stanley W. Jacob, M.D., and Robert Herachler, an organic chemist, discovered that DMSO solvent had the ability to penetrate the skin, enter the blood stream, and become systemic (affect the body as a whole). DMSO solvent demonstrated at least five basic medicinal properties when applied topically. In experimental animals, DMSO solvent caused near-sightedness. This has not occurred in humans.

1. DMSO solvent is bactiostatic at 20% concentration - That means that the growth and multiplication of bacteria is inhibited.

2. DMSO solvent is a vasodilator - It enlarges small veins and capillaries, increasing blood flow to an area.

3. DMSO solvent has analgesic properties - this means that pain will be relieved. You may note some pain relief; however the time sequence many vary.

4. DMSO solvent has anti-inflammatory activities. - An anti-inflammatory agent relieves the swelling and the inflammation of arthritis, bursitis, tendonitis, and other soft-tissue injuries (Cortisone is a steroid which is an anti-inflammatory agent. DMSO is *not* a steroid).

5. DMSO solvent will soften scar tissue.

Present status of DMSO Solvent:

DMSO solvent is approved by the FDA for use in interstitial cys-[titis, a disabling inflammation of the urinary bladder.

Side Effects:

The side effects of DMSO solvent include *garlicky* breath and skin irritation which may be manifested as a fine, red rash or *sunburn-like* blisters. An occasional user has been allergic to DMSO solvent. Many users feel only warmth.

Proper Application and Use:

Initial application should be a 50/50 dilution with water to suppress side effects. This can be adjusted to suit individuals. If intense skin side-effects occur, a 50% solvent with 50% vitamin E oil is a working alternative. For optimum results, DMSO solvent should be applied directly to the area of discomfort because DMSO solvent penetrates the skin and becomes systemic, with benefits that will be felt in other parts of the body.

Important note: Because DMSO solvent takes material into the system, the skin must be perfectly clean and all cosmetics, body lotions, aerosol sprays and any topical medications should be avoided over the area of application for at least three hours after the last application.

About 25 to 35 minutes is required for penetration. The skin should not be washed or wiped until penetration occurs.

Keep in mind that DMSO solvent is both a drug and a good solvent. It can remove certain paints and varnishes in your home. The industrial grade of DMSO solvent, which is less than 90% pure, is dangerous to use as a drug. It can dissolve or soften certain materials (clothing and accessories) such as rayon, polyvinyl chlorides, polyurethanes, meth acrylics and acrylics. DMSO solvent is safe with cotton, wool, nylon, leather, and polyesters. No material that may be dissolved by DMSO solvent should be allowed to touch the area to which the DMSO solvent is applied until total penetration (3 hours) has occurred.

10 Minute Facial

This is included here because of the overwhelming number of requests for it I have received over the years.

Recipe: 3 Tablespoons of Plain Yogurt

1 Teaspoon of Fullers Earth

1 Egg White

1 Teaspoon of Honey

Mix together all ingredients, leave on face for 10 minutes and rinse. Then stand back - admire and wait for the caresses. You'll be as pretty as me!

Chapter 10

Words to Live By

I wanted to include these words to be helpful to everyone that might find a benefit from them as we travel through life and might need some helpful words that I have shared with my listeners to help them through life's trials. – Dave

These stories are valuable to all that read them. Some may seem familiar, but I still wanted them included in this book. I considered them important for all my readers and I hope you feel inspired by them.

All I Ever Really Needed to Know

Most of what I really need to know about how to live, what to do, and how to be, I learned in kindergarten. Wisdom was not at the top of the graduate school mountain, but there in the sandbox at nursery school. These are the things I learned:

Share everything. Play fair. Don't hit people.

Put things back where you found them.

Clean up your own mess.

Don't take things that aren't yours.

Say you're sorry when you hurt somebody.

Wash your hands before you eat.
Flush.
Warm cookies and cold milk are good for you.
Live a balanced life.
Learn some and think some and draw, paint, sing, dance, and play, and work some every day.
Take a nap every afternoon.
When you go out into the world, watch for traffic, hold hands, and stick together.
Be aware of wonder.
Remember the little seed in the plastic cup. The roots grow down and the plant grows up and nobody really knows how or why, but we are all like that.
Goldfish and hamsters and white mice and even the little seed in the plastic cup - they all die. So do we.
Remember the book about Dick and Jane and the first word you learned, the biggest word of all: *LOOK*. Everything you need to know is in there somewhere. The Golden Rule and love and basic sanitation; Ecology and politics and sane living.
Think of what a better world it would be if we all - the whole world - had cookies and milk about 3 o'clock every afternoon and then lay down with our blankets for a nap. Or if we had a basic policy in our nation and other nations to always put things back where we found them and cleaned up our own messes. And it is still true, no matter how old you are, when you go out into the world, it is best to hold hands and stick together.

- Author unknown

Purple & Red Hats

When I am an old lady, I shall wear purple,
With a red hat, which doesn't go and doesn't suit me.
And I shall spend my pension on brandy and summer gloves,
And satin sandals, and say we have no money for butter.
I shall sit down on the pavement when I am tired,
And gobble up samples in shops and press alarm bells.
And run my stick along public railings,
And make up for the sobriety of my youth.
I shall go out in my slippers in the rain,
And pick the flowers in other people's gardens,
And learn to spit.

But maybe I ought to practice a little now
So people who know me are not too shocked and surprised
When suddenly I am old and start to wear purple.
-Authored by Jenny Joseph, a British poet

I'm a Senior Citizen!

-I'm the life of the party . . . even if it lasts 'til 8:30 p.m.

-I'm usually interested in going home before I get to where I am going.

-I'm good for at least an hour on a trip without my aspirins, antacids, etc.

-I'm the first one to find the bathroom everywhere I go.

-I'm awake many hours before my body lets me get up.

-I'm smiling all the time because I can't hear a word you are saying.

-I'm very good at telling stories over and over and over and over.

-I'm aware that other people's grandchildren are not as smart as mine.

-I'm so cared for: long-term care; eye care; private care; dental care.

-I'm not grouchy, I just don't like traffic, waiting, children and politicians.

-I'm sure everything I can't find is in a secure place.

-I'm wrinkled, saggy and lumpy, and that's just my left leg.

-I'm having trouble remembering simple words like . . . uh . . .

-I'm now spending more time with my pillows than with my mate.

-I'm walking more (to the bathroom) and enjoying it less.

-I'm sure they are making adults much younger these days.

-I'm in the *initial* state of my golden years.

-I'm wondering: if you are only as old as you feel, how could I be alive at 150?

-I'm anti everything now: anti-fat, anti-smoke, anti-noise, anti-inflammatory.

-I'm supporting all movements now . . . by eating bran, prunes and raisins.

-I'm a walking storeroom of facts . . . I've just lost the key!

-I'm a senior citizen and I think I am having the time of my life!
-Author Unknown

A Poem by Mary Frye

Mrs. Mary Frye, a 78 year old poet definitely had a talent for moving people with her words, and touch their deepest emotions in a time of crisis. One of her poems, jotted down with no motive beyond offering comfort to a friend, has become an American classic, used in countless funeral services, passed along from person to person, translated and used in foreign lands, and even incorporated into television drama.

Here's her original text that has moved so many, for so long:

"Do not stand at my grave and weep,
I am not there. I do not sleep.
I am in a thousand winds that blow,
I am the softly falling snow.
I am the gentle showers of rain,
I am the fields of ripening grain.
I am in the morning hush,
I am in the graceful rush
Of beautiful birds in circling flight,
I am the star shine of the night.
I am in the flowers that bloom,
I am in the quiet room,
I am the birds that sing,
I am in each lovely thing.
Do not stand at my grave and cry,
I am not there. I do not die."

Mary Frye said she was orphaned at age three and went to work to support herself at age 12. "I educated myself through the library. There was a library right across the street and I think I read about everything there. Anybody who wants an education can get it. You can always educate yourself," she said.

-From an article authored by Richard K. Shull
posted in The Indianapolis News, 6/9/1983

Chapter 11

Pearls of Wisdom

I thought you might enjoy some helpful hints on how to handle some of the challenges life holds for us. This chapter includes some quotes I used on my radio show. They generated a lot of conversation with my listeners. I wanted to share these with you, as well as some flourishes on the rest of one's life journey.

How to Do Almost Anything . . . Better

1. How to answer a tough question: Be direct. Come armed with the facts; keep your sense of humor, don't take it personally - and never, ever lie.

- Dee Dee Myers, White House Press Secretary

2. How to take a great photograph: Move around and don't be afraid to get close to your subject. With children, get down on their level. Create a sense of perspective. For instance, use a foreground object such as a tree branch in a landscape picture. Make your subject feel comfortable. Then look for that special emotion to make the picture come alive. Shoot, shoot, shoot. Then analyze your pictures and apply what you've learned to your next roll.

- Tipper Gore, wife of Vice President Al Gore and

former photographer for The Tennessean

3.   How to build a preschooler's self-confidence: Avoid using words like *good* and *bad.* When you say something is good, your child has to live up to that standard in the future. Instead, describe how you feel about what your child has done. Or ask her how *she* feels. When she shows you a piece of artwork, instead of saying "that's good," say "that makes me feel wonderful. Let's put it on the fridge," or say, "Are you happy with that drawing? What do you like about it?" By soliciting your child's opinion, you're telling her that what she thinks is just as important as what you think.

- Sheryl Leach, creator of "Barney"

4.   How to criticize politely: First, wait until you are asked for your opinion. Second, when the request is made, figure out whether it is really a plea for the unadorned truth. Many inquiries, such as, "Do I look all right?" and "Did I make a complete fool of myself?" are requests for reassurance and must be treated as such. Third, if the request *is* for the unadorned truth, adorn it anyway.

- Judith Martin, Miss Manners

5.   How to avoid jet lag: Change into sweats in the airplane bathroom and put on heaps of moisturizer. Drink about three glasses of water and a cup of herbal tea. I like rose hip tea because it has a lot of vitamin C. When dinner arrives, eat only the salads and light food. Skip the red meat. Spray Evian on your face to keep it moist throughout the trip. Try to sleep during the movie. Just before landing, wash your face, brush your teeth, and change your clothes.

- Nicole Kidman, Australian born actress who frequently makes the 15-hour trip from Los Angeles to Sydney

6.   How to Stop a Rumor: I don't think you *can* stop a rumor, but usually the less said the better. The best way to slow it down is not to repeat it yourself. If the rumor is about you, consider heading the gossip off at the pass by confronting it head-on and setting the record straight.

- Liz Smith nationally syndicated gossip columnist

7.   How to travel with a baby:

a. Skip those six-cities-in-five-days tours. Plan a one-stop vacation.

b. Don't under-pack. Remember essentials such as wipes, sealable plastic bags, snacks if baby is on solids, toilet and cabinet locks, outlet covers, and a locked bag of medical and grooming necessities.

c. If you're flying, bring a car seat. Booking an extra seat is expensive, but much safer and more comfortable than holding a baby on your lap.

d. Baby-proof your destination. Check that crib slats are no more than 2-3/8 inches apart, look out for open windows, electrical cords, and poisonous plants.

- Heidi E. Hurkoff and Arlene Eisenberg, authors of
What To Expect When You're Expecting and
What to Expect: The Toddler Years

8. How to write a love note: Keep it short, adorable, and totally about him. Talk about his smile, legs, storytelling ability, etc. Leave yourself and the great love affair out of the mix.

- Helen Gurley Brown, editor in chief of Cosmopolitan

9. How to create the best bouffant (that's volume hair for our younger readers): "I rat the tar out of it, spray the hell out of it. I get it up there and defy gravity."

- Gail Huitt, hairdresser to Texas Governor Ann Richards

10. How to build a wardrobe from scratch:

First, review what you own and discard anything that doesn't fit, you haven't worn in a while, or don't see yourself wearing in the near future.

Second, Select a neutral color such as black or camel and center your wardrobe around it. Make sure what you purchase is multi-functional, meaning with a quick change of accessories you can go from day to evening or by adding jeans and casual shoes, you're ready for the weekend. Tops can reflect a more playful, spirited attitude.

Third, Invest in a good cashmere wool or silk linen blend blazer.

- Adrienne Vittadini designer

11. How to be a great cook: Do a lot of reading. Take some cooking courses. Find some friends who are good cooks and offer to help them, peel potatoes, whatever. Just spend time in the kitchen with them learning how to do all the dog work. Take food seriously as an art and pleasure. Cook.

- Julia Child world-renowned chef and cookbook author

12. How to survive a loving mother: It's not easy. There's nothing more difficult to handle than someone with good intentions. But instead of getting upset, learn to say, "I know you love me, but back off a bit." If that doesn't work, take her shopping and then ditch her.

- Melissa Rivers, MTV feature reporter and
daughter of Joan Rivers

13. How to make love to a man forever: You have to maintain a level of romance outside the bedroom so that when you get into bed you'll feel sexy and want to make love. You can do this by really listening to him when he talks, calling him during the day and telling him how much you care for him, and even tucking a little love note in his pocket or briefcase. When he comes home, he'll want to make love to you, too.

- Sydney Biddle Barrows, former Mayflower Madam

14. How do you grow your hair to your feet: The same way you grow it to you waist -- only more.

- Crystal Gayle, singer

15. How to boost a man's self-esteem: When you're talking to him, never let your eyes roam. I don't care if a flying saucer careens into the room and two little green men get out. Stay absolutely focused.

- Georgette Mosbacher, founder of Exclusives cosmetics, and
author of Feminine Force

16. How to make a book: You need paper and pictures. And you have to know what color the book is going to be: black and white or just color. It's hard to find the words. You have to figure out if you want to say *play* or *AIDS* or *pink* or *yellow*.

- Camera Ashe, 6-year-old daughter of the late Arthur Ashe and
author of Daddy and Me

-All excerpts taken from an unknown magazine article written by Alexis Sinclair.

You Know You're Getting Old When:

Candidates for public office are your age or younger;
You decide to look elegant every day at the supermarket;
You start putting up with men who smoke cigars;
You ask people to guess your age;
You stop asking for love and start giving it;
Your son starts treating you with respect;
Your son goes off to college and reminds you not to forget to write, even if it's only a small check;
You are no longer in terror of the headwaiter;
You wonder why you've never been asked to an orgy;
You start talking to your sister again;
The candlelit tables are no longer romantic because you can't read the menu.

-Author Unknown

Chapter 12

The Miracle of Birth

The author of the following poem was a sweet, thoughtful and long-time listener of mine, and for my birthday, she sent me this poem as a gift. I think she went a little overboard, but I thought you might enjoy the tone and the sentiment and her amazing talent for poetry, even when it came to writing about yours truly! She managed to even make *me* blush.

This seemed to me to be an excellent way to end the book.

The legend of the Mixed Up Stork, St. Patrick's Day . . . In Old New York

We know it's, "Happy Birthday, Dave" and many more to be.
But you wondered how it started? Well, listen then, to me.
Once upon St Patrick's Day, on March seventeen,
A great big bird with long, long legs and a bundle wrapped in green
Was standing in a Cabbage Patch amidst the Birds and Bees,
Awaiting flight instructions and directions, if you please.
When the Flight Director gave him the "Go Ahead,"
He was airborne with a mighty *Whoosh* and on his way he sped!
With his huge white wings a-flapping and a smile upon his beak

As he soared above Long Island Sound his 'Package' sprung a leak.

The poor old Stork was puzzled, didn't quite know what to do.

The bundle that he toted didn't bill or didn't coo

But emitted rasping noises, sometimes high and sometimes low,

That sounded just like static on your basic radio.

And when the clock struck 6 a.m., the stork was shocked to see

His little green clad bundle start screeching "Reveille."

Now all the other babies that he'd delivered thus

We're paragons of babyhood and never made a fuss.

So the scraggly old stork wondered, "What's with this kid?

How come they gave *me* this job . . . Was it something I did?"

He sputtered and he stammered, let go a few choice words (*#!%* * !!!)

Equivalent in bird talk to "This is for the birds!"

He was hedgehopping Port Chester, perplexed as he could be,

Fearing for his reputation and muttering, "Why me?"

He was growing empty-headed from circling the town

And thinking up excuses to keep from 'touching down.'

You think all this is different? More different than you think?

The bird was so embarrassed that he turned three shades of pink.

He tried to hide behind the trees. Sure, he was flying low,

He prayed that he would make it. He had four more miles to go.

The other storks flew 'round him and asked with jaundiced eye,

"What's with it with that baby? That's not a normal cry!"

It could be a great malfunctioning or merely just a quirk,

The storks all tried to shush him, but their methods didn't work.

The raucous notes of "Reveille" still rang out loud and clear.

The bird was truly mortified! Why, all New York could hear!

Most babies hold a rattle but this one was a winner.

He clutched within his grubby fist a radio antenna!

He simple couldn't take it! He simply must save face!

So he landed in a hurry at a homey looking place.

The mailbox stated "MAYNARD" so he pulled the lid of tin,

And 'tho it was a real tight squeeze he shoved his bundle in!

He flapped off in a hurry thinking, "Boy, that sure was close!

They better never give me another one of those!"

But he didn't have to worry or pay it any mind.
You bet your life they broke the mold! That kid's one of a kind!
When unsuspecting Father Maynard went out to get the mail,
He found a subdued bundle, quite soggy, meek and pale.
He was truly flabbergasted and most surprised to see
That rightfully the tag affixed was labeled "C.O.D."
Father Maynard was elated! He began to rant and rave,
"This kid will be on radio! I think we'll call him 'Dave.'
And 'tho I shouldn't brag at all or even slightly boast,
This kid is going places! He'll be a talk show host!
Although he doesn't look like much (if you'll excuse the dig),
This kid's got what it takes to be "the start of something big!"
Now that was many years ago. How many, I won't say,
But that is why we're gathered here to celebrate today.
If you should meet that mixed up stork he'll tell you he's re-
tired,
He couldn't take another 'trip.' (I heard that he was fired!)
No matter what the reason was or what the case may be,
That stork, somehow, is strangely drawn to WBZ.
As he flies around in circles he can't shake it from his mind.
It's become his personal albatross . . . the multi-media kind.
So now ends my narration, a "legend in its time,"
The start of David Maynard, in story and in rhyme.
St. Patrick's Day, March 17th, in Port Chester, New York,
Little Davie was delivered by a crazy, mixed up stork,
Spoutin' Irish blarney that would shame a leprechaun,
As naked as a jaybird with nearly nothin' on!
Oops! Wait until I'm finished before you hide your face . . .
He did have a bright green diaper held in its rightful place,
With diaper pins initialed, "D.H.M." in solid gold.
That's *really* how it all began! (Or so I have been told!)

- Quine Aalto, long life fan, Millis, MA, 1982

Addendum

Dave Maynard's Awards

Salvation Army "Tambourine" Award -- 1977
Community Auditions, "1st Place, Tap Dancing" – 1980
Delta Airlines "Flying Colonel" -- 1980
Senator Edward M. Kennedy, Letter of Recognition -- 1983
Boston Children's Hospital "Recognition for Fundraising" -- 1983
Wonderland Park "Appreciation Bowl" -- 1985
Boston Children's Hospital "Revere Bowl Appreciation" -- 1987
United Cerebral Palsy "Distinguished Service" Award -- 1987
Mayor Raymond Flynn Proclamation "Dave Maynard Day"
March 17, 1989
Board of Selectmen, Maynard, MA "Dave Maynard Day"
March 17, 1989
Arthritis Foundation Committee "Recognition" -- 1991
Boston University College of Communication
"Distinguished Alumni" -- 1991
The Scheppens Eye Research Institute
"Swim for Sight" Letter of Recognition -- 1993
Proclaimed *"Honorary Citizen of Dublin, Ireland"* March 17, 1993
Boston Children's Hospital "Honorary Life Overseer" -- 1995
Boston Children's Hospital "Chairman's Award" -- 1996
March of Dimes "AIR Lifetime Achievement" -- 1999
Emerson College "Rho Delta Omega" Award, 60th Reunion -- 2008

Massachusetts Broadcasters Association "Broadcaster of the Year"
-- 1999
WBZ "Wall of Fame", 41 Years. -- 2009
New England/Massachusetts Broadcasters "Hall of Fame", 50-year
career, 2009

www.ingramcontent.com/pod-product-compliance
Lightning Source LLC
Chambersburg PA
CBHW060746100426
42813CB00032B/3419/J